FEBRUARY 50 COLORING PAGES FOR OLDER KIDS RELAXATION

SHIH CHIEN HUA

PUBLISHED BY:
SHIH CHIEN HUA
Copyright © 2018

SEABIRD SHOP >50FOR

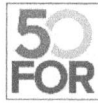

FB FAN PAGE

Disclaimer
The information contained in this book is for general information purposes only. The information is provided by the authors and while we endeavor to keep the information up to date and correct, we make no representations or warranties of any kind, express or implied, about the completeness, accuracy, reliability, suitability or availability with respect to the book or the information, products, services, or related graphics contained in the book for any purpose. Any reliance you place on such information is therefore strictly at your own risk.

FEBRUARY 1ST

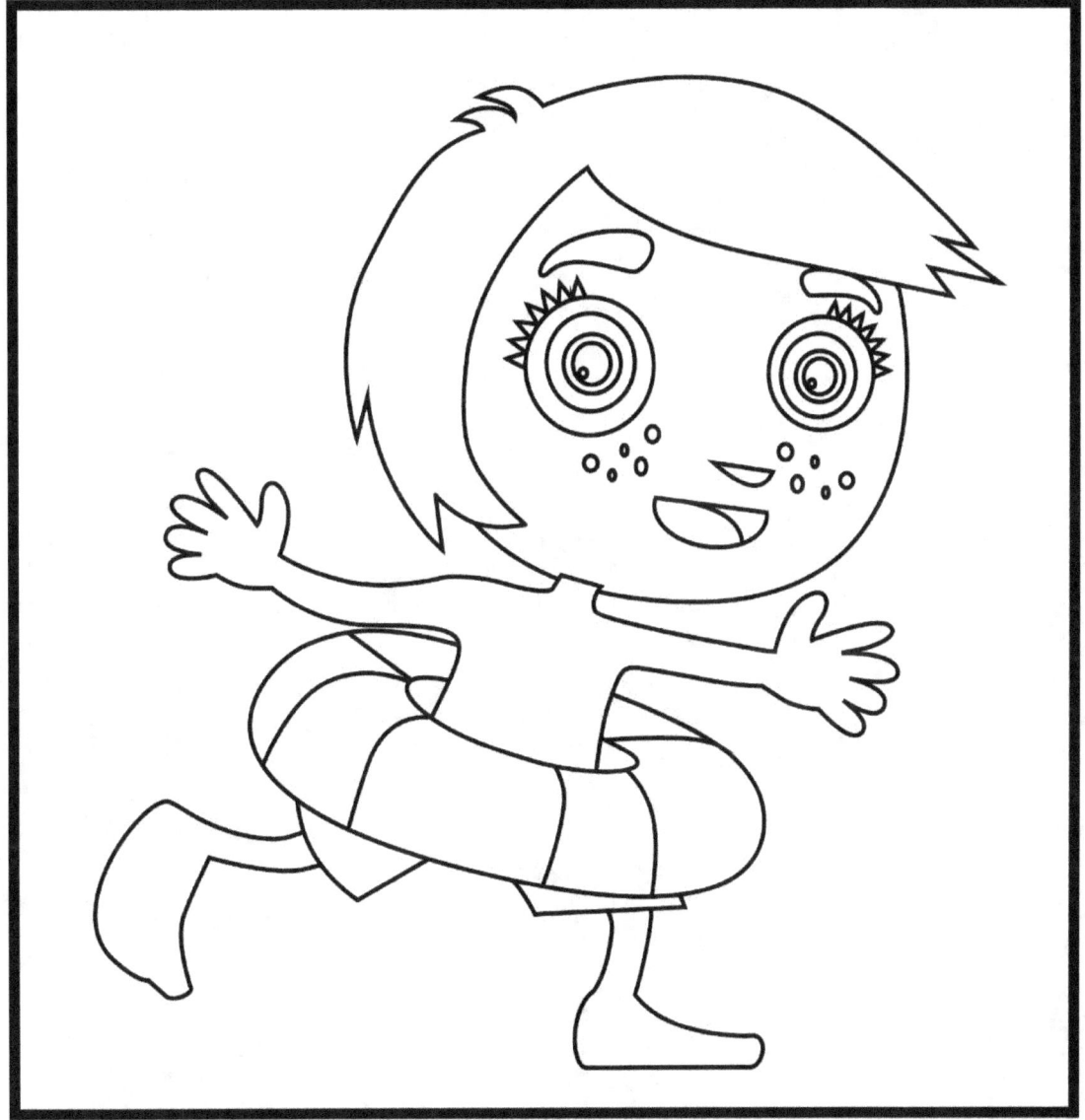

note:

_____

_____

_____

FEBRUARY 2ND

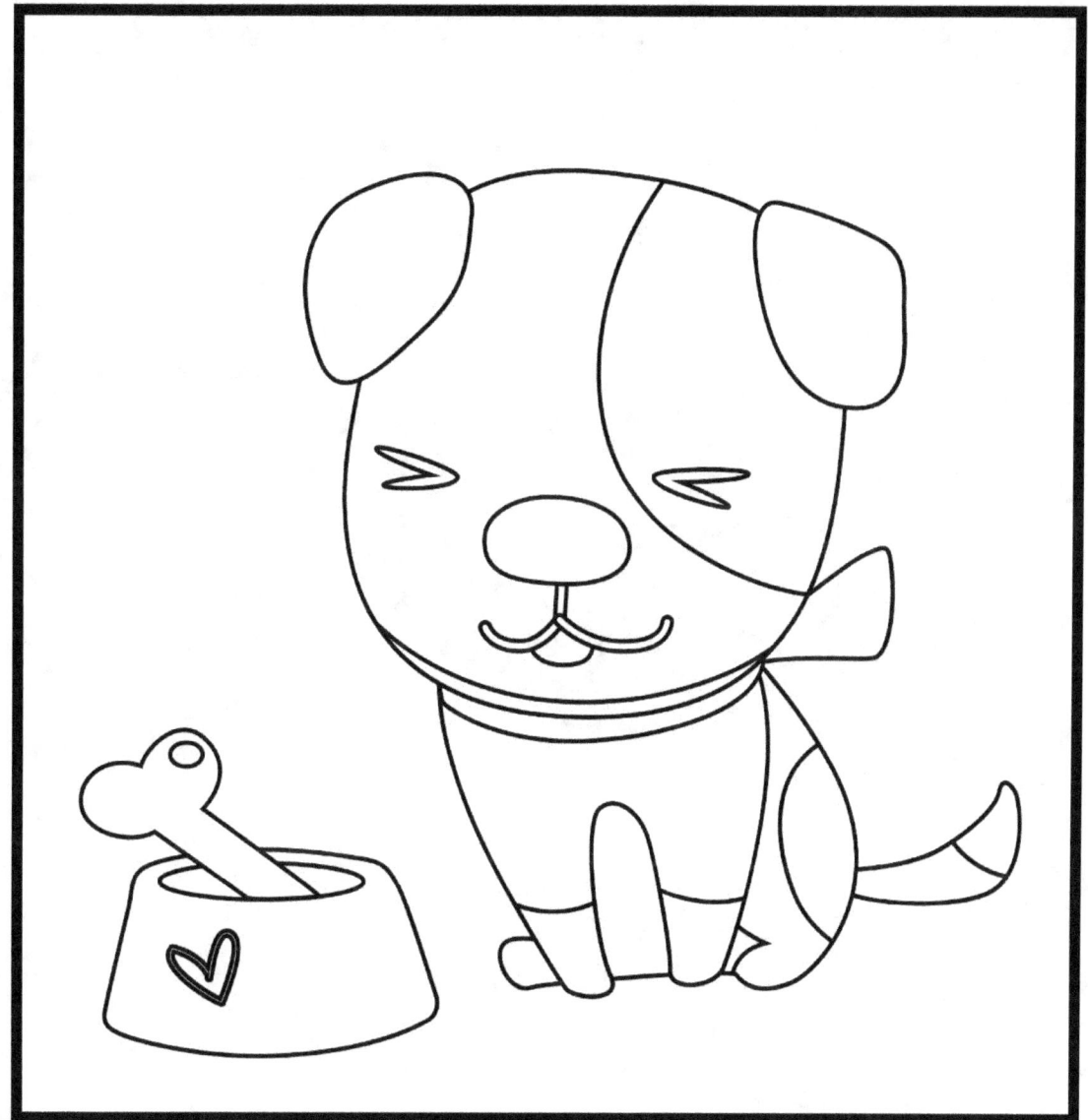

note:

_____

_____

_____

FEBRUARY 3ND

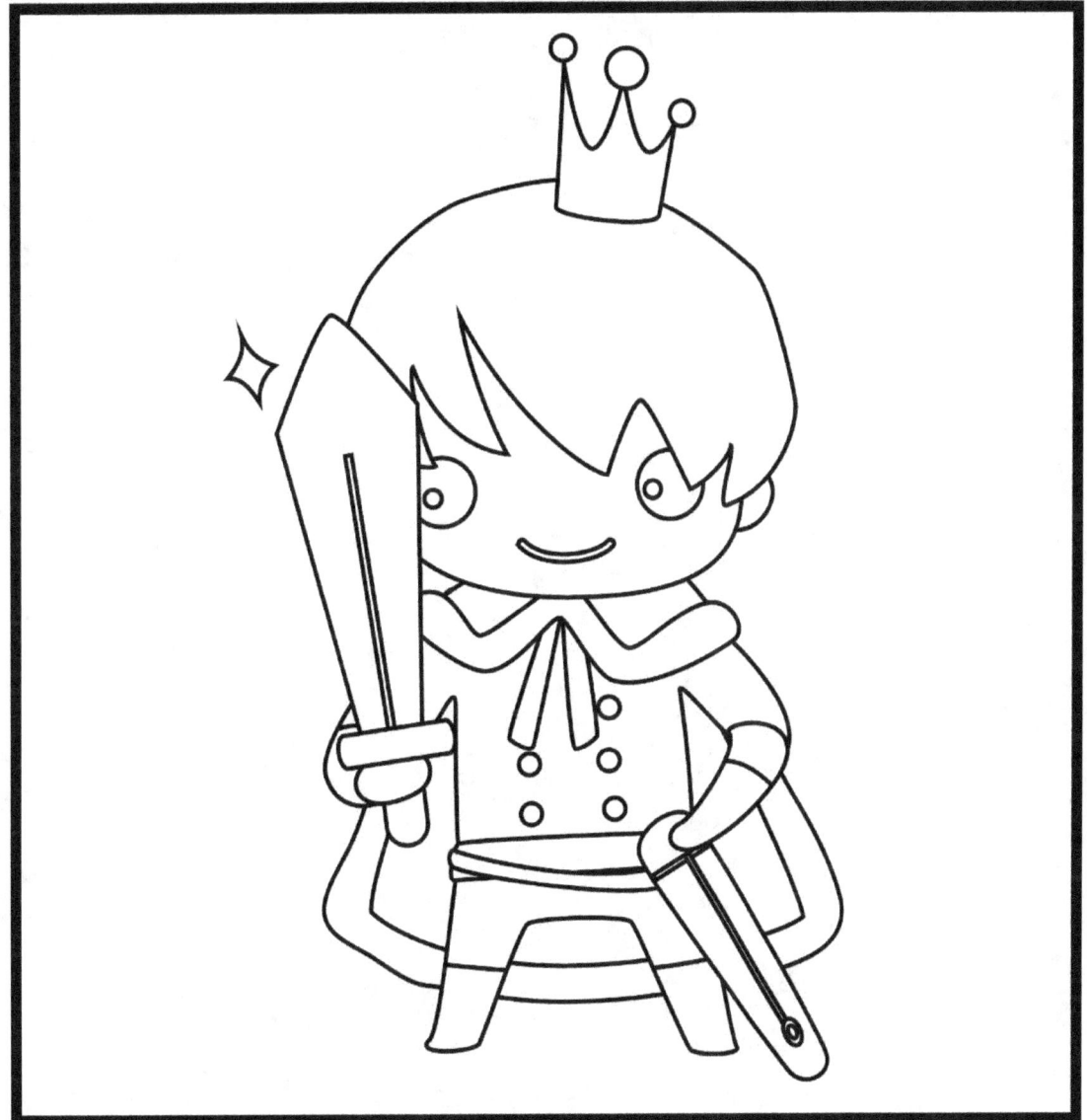

note:

_____

_____

_____

FEBRUARY 4ND

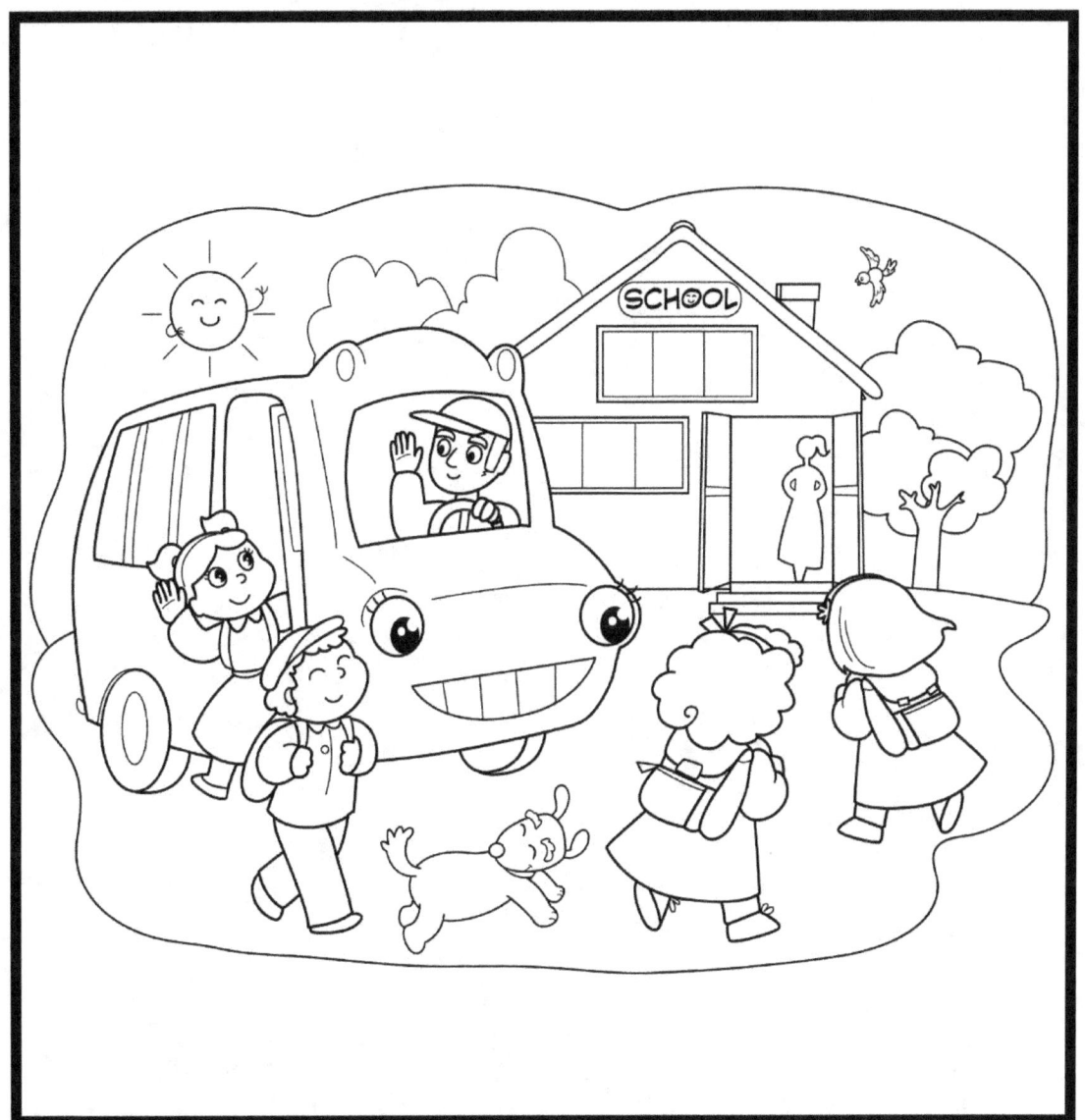

note:

_____

_____

_____

FEBRUARY 5ND

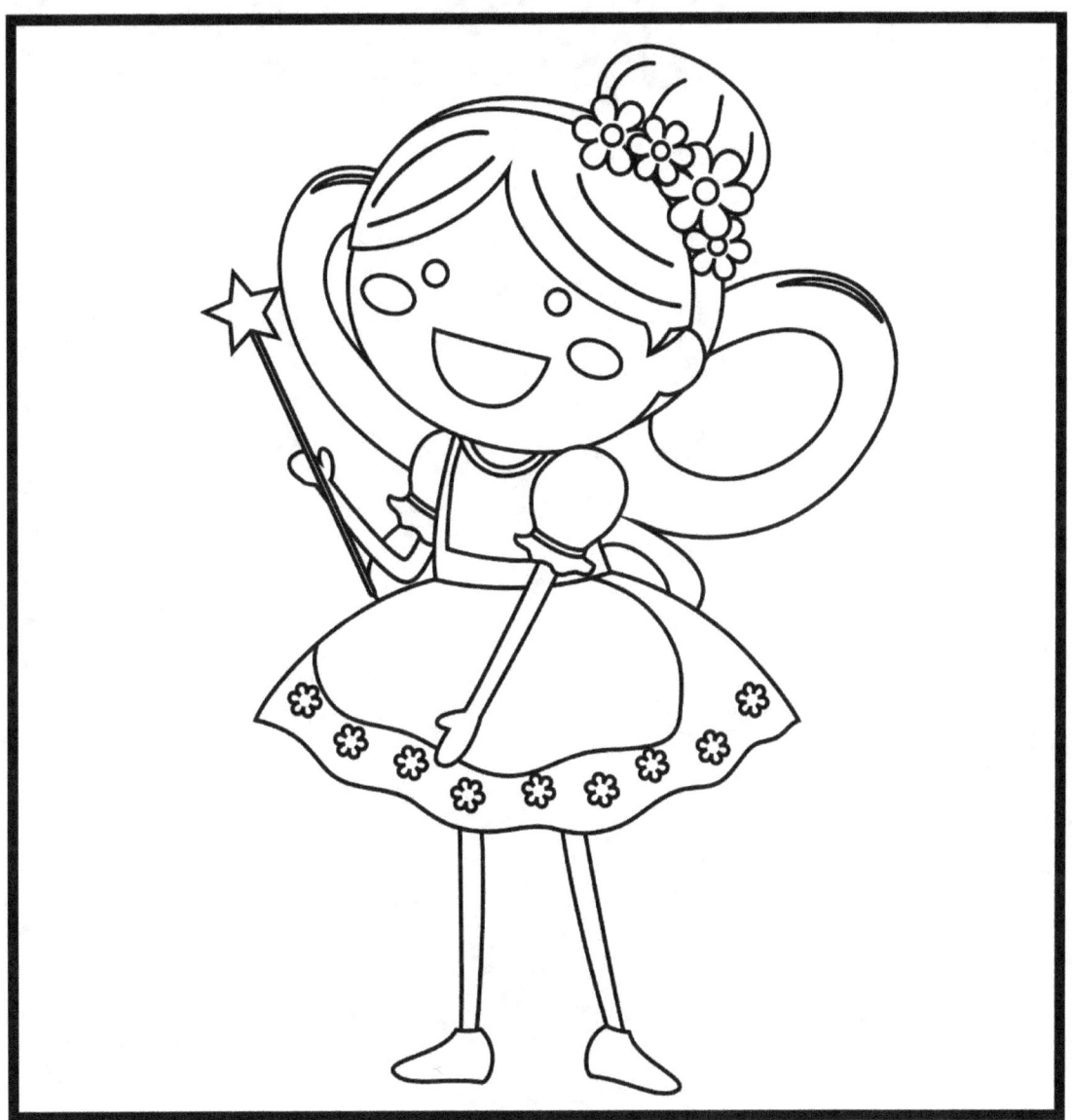

note:

_____

_____

_____

FEBRUARY 6ND

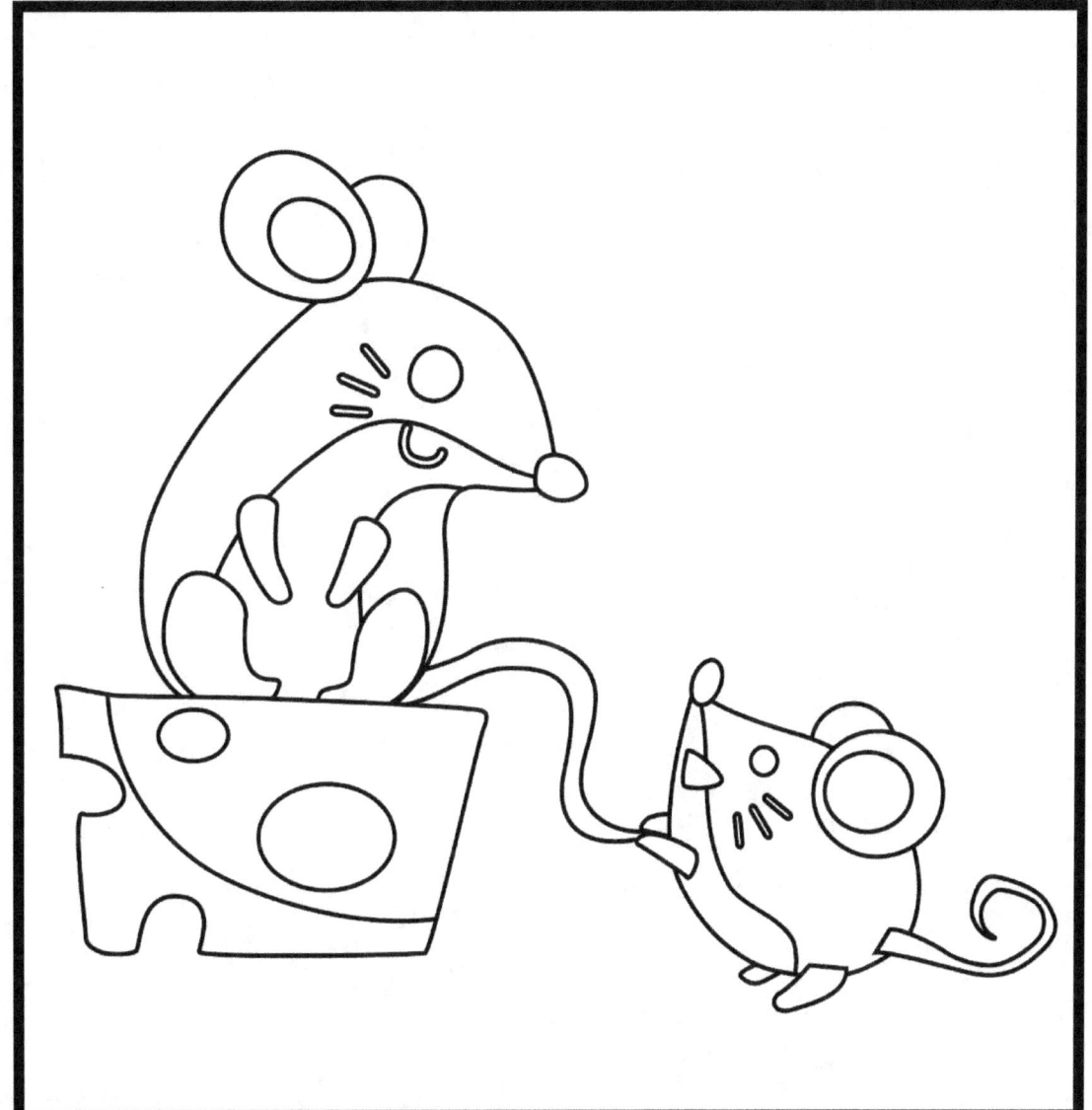

note:

_____

_____

_____

FEBRUARY 7ND

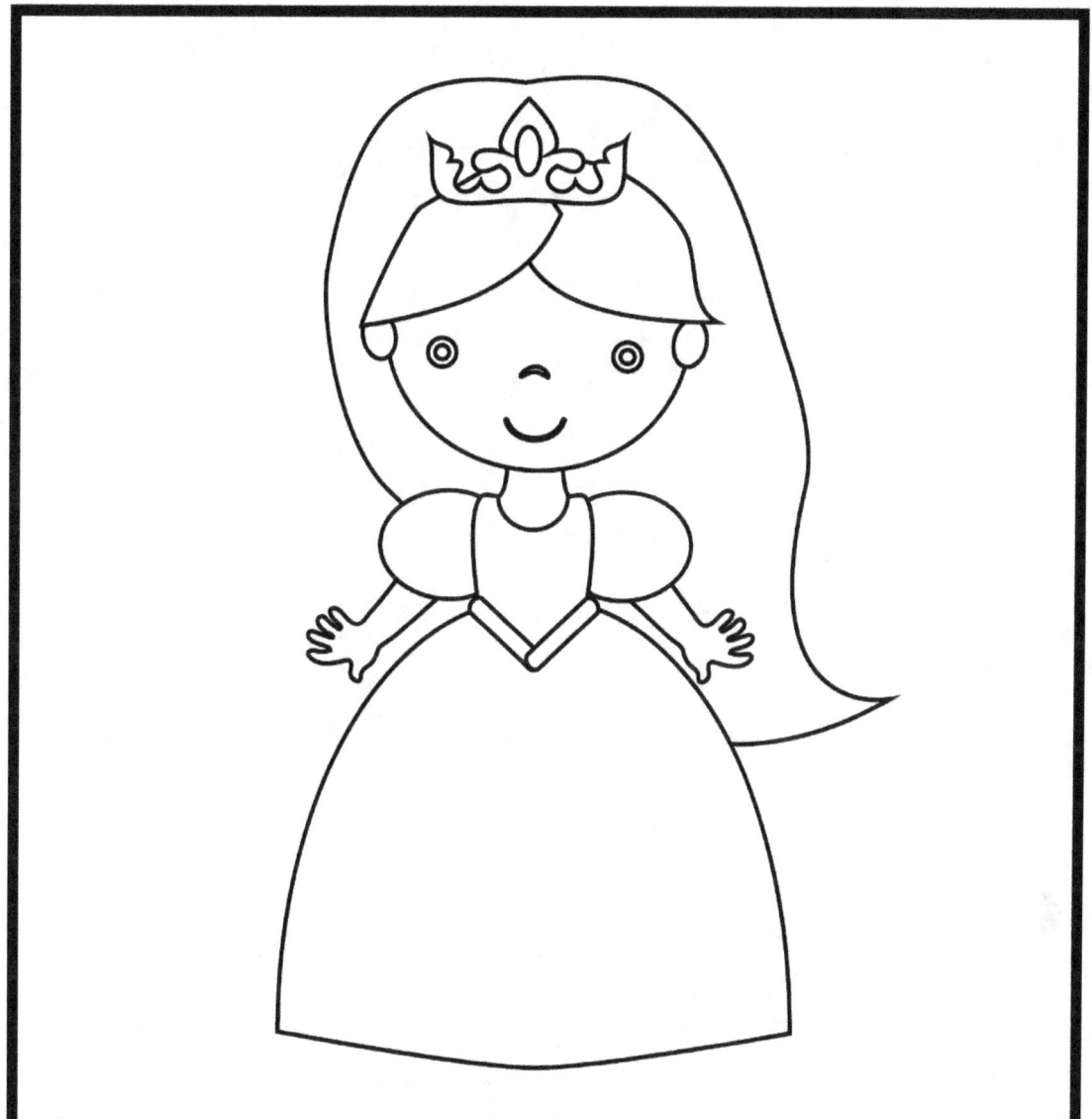

note:

_____

_____

_____

FEBRUARY 8ND

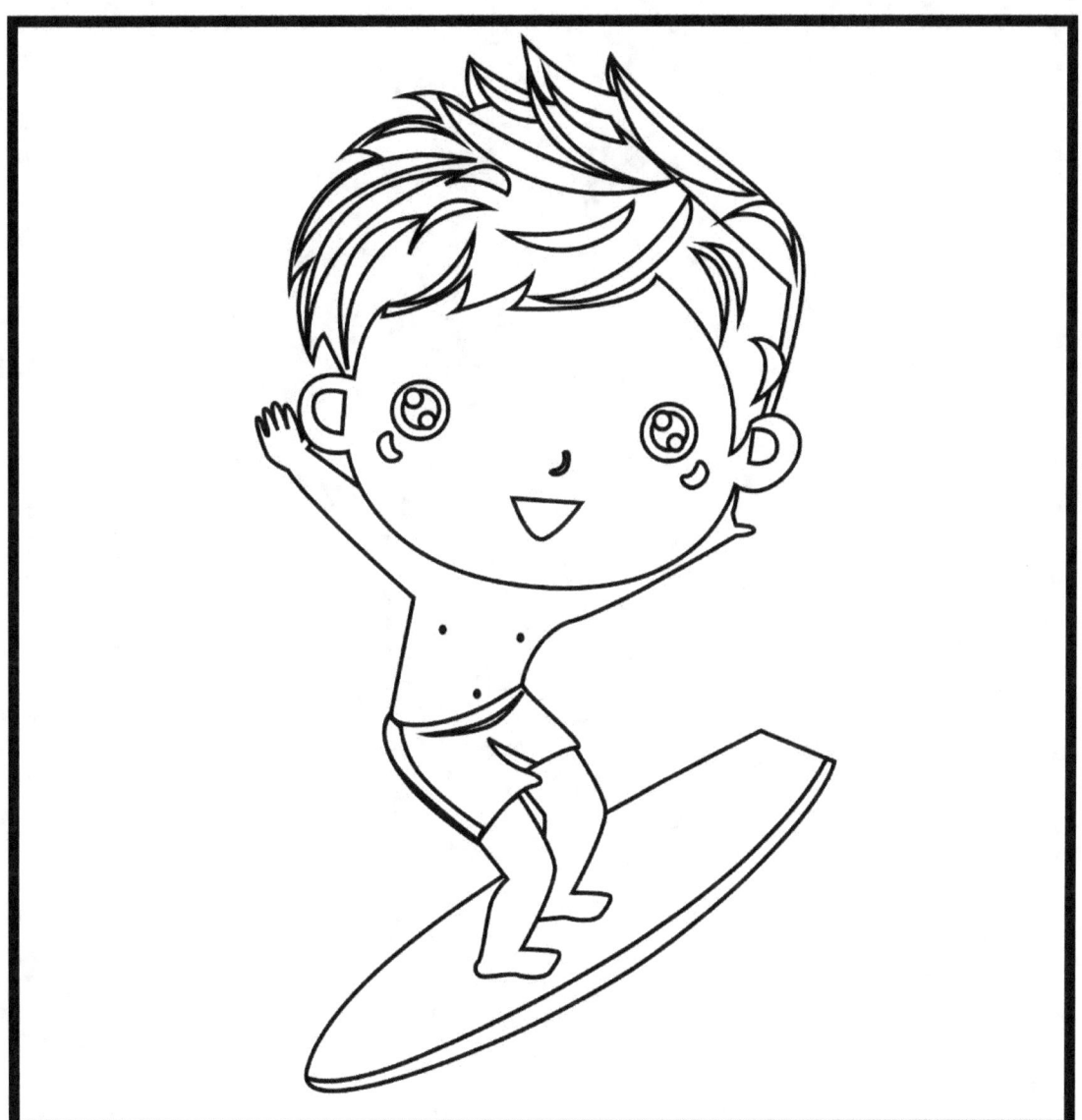

note:

_____

_____

_____

FEBRUARY 9ND

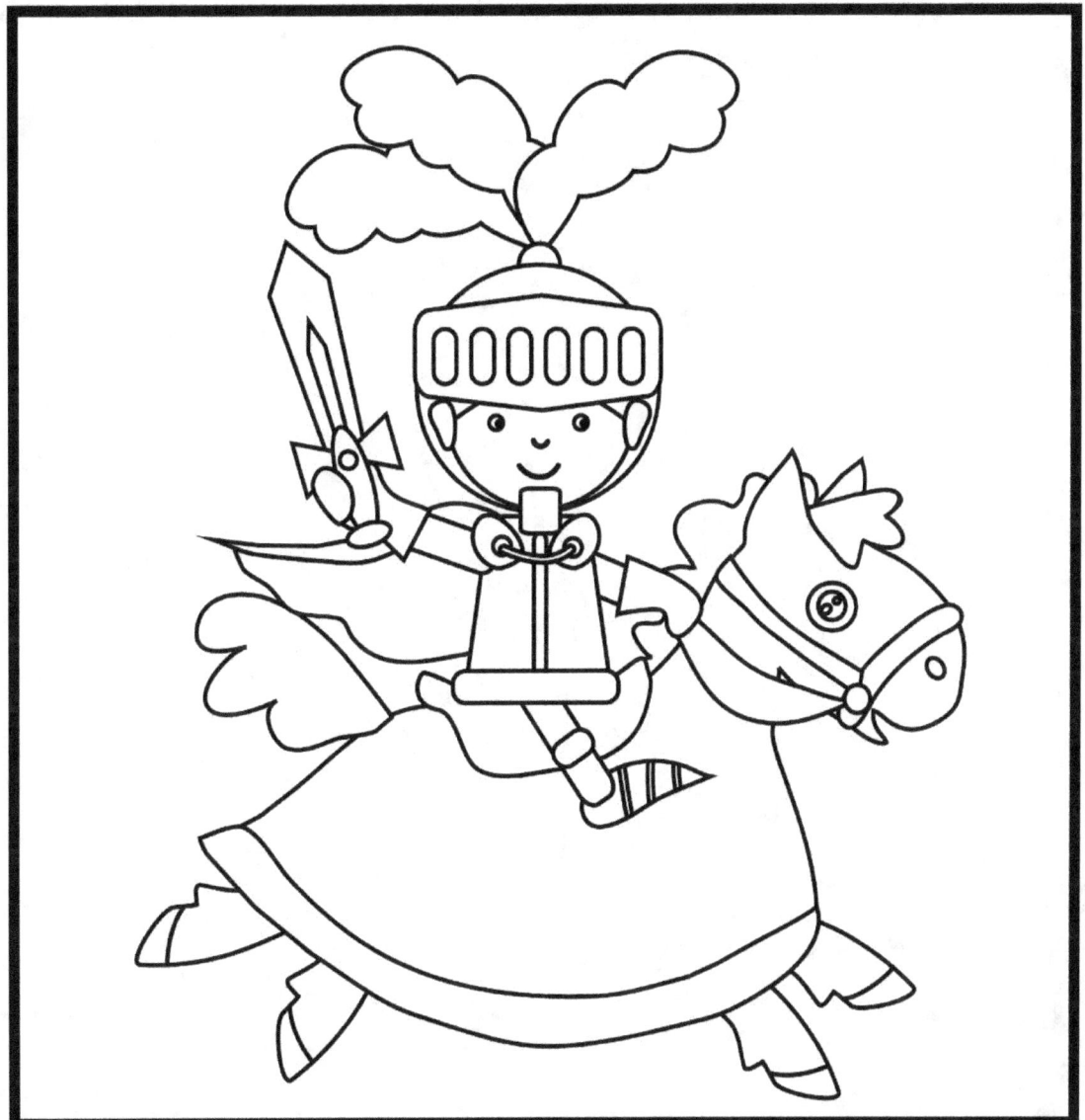

note:

_____

_____

_____

FEBRUARY 10TH

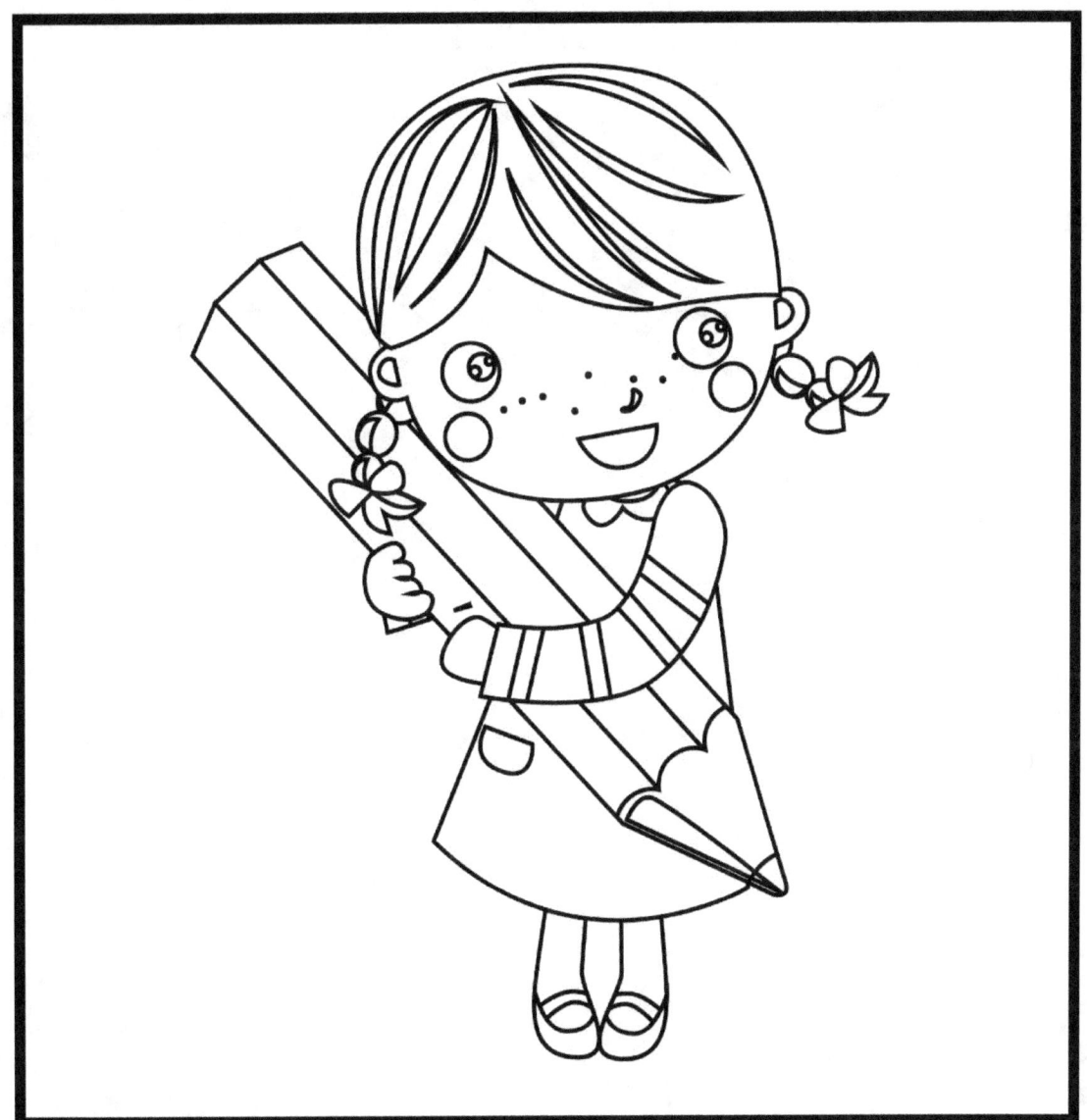

note:

_____

_____

_____

FEBRUARY 11TH

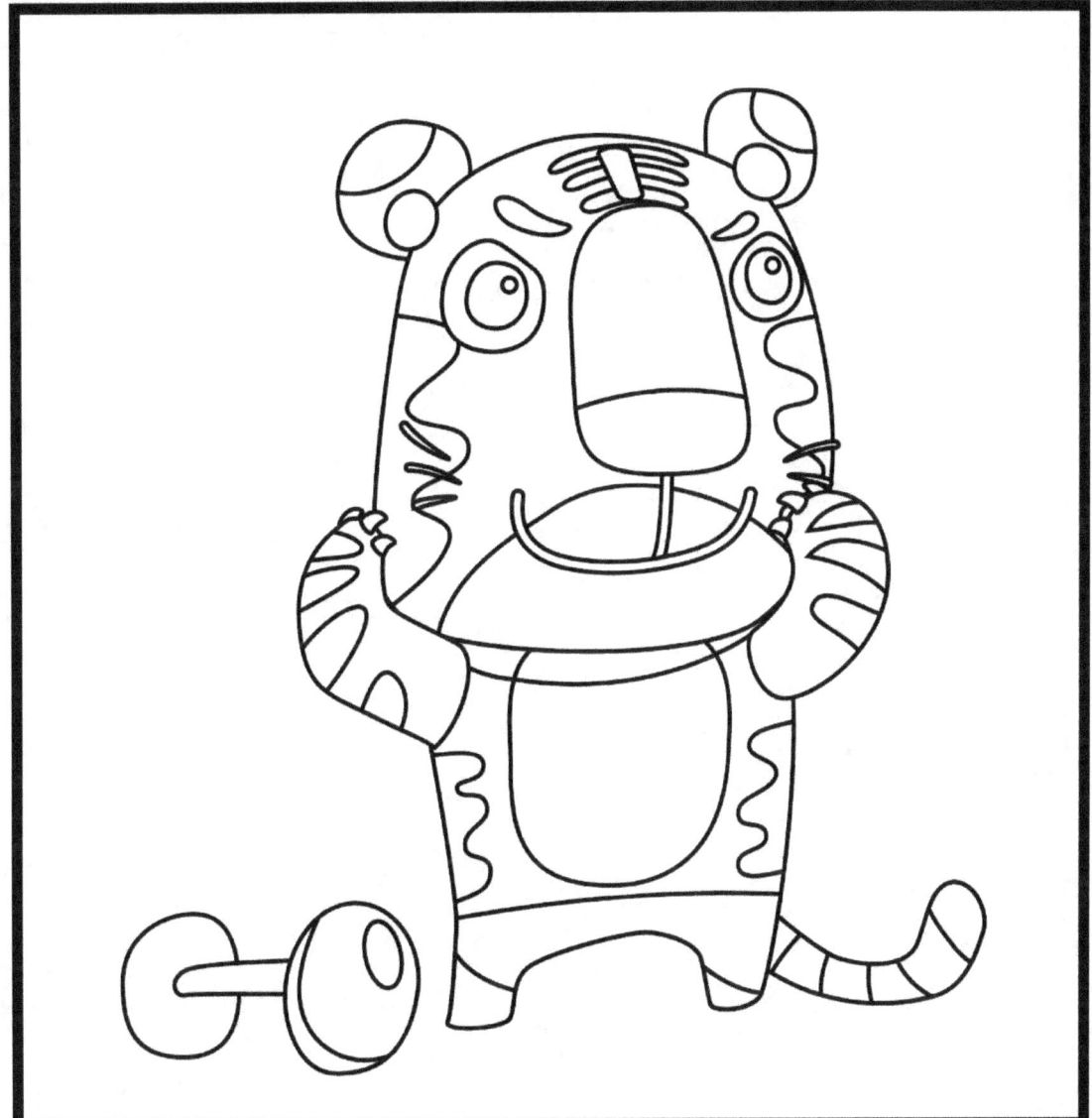

note:

_____

_____

_____

FEBRUARY 12TH

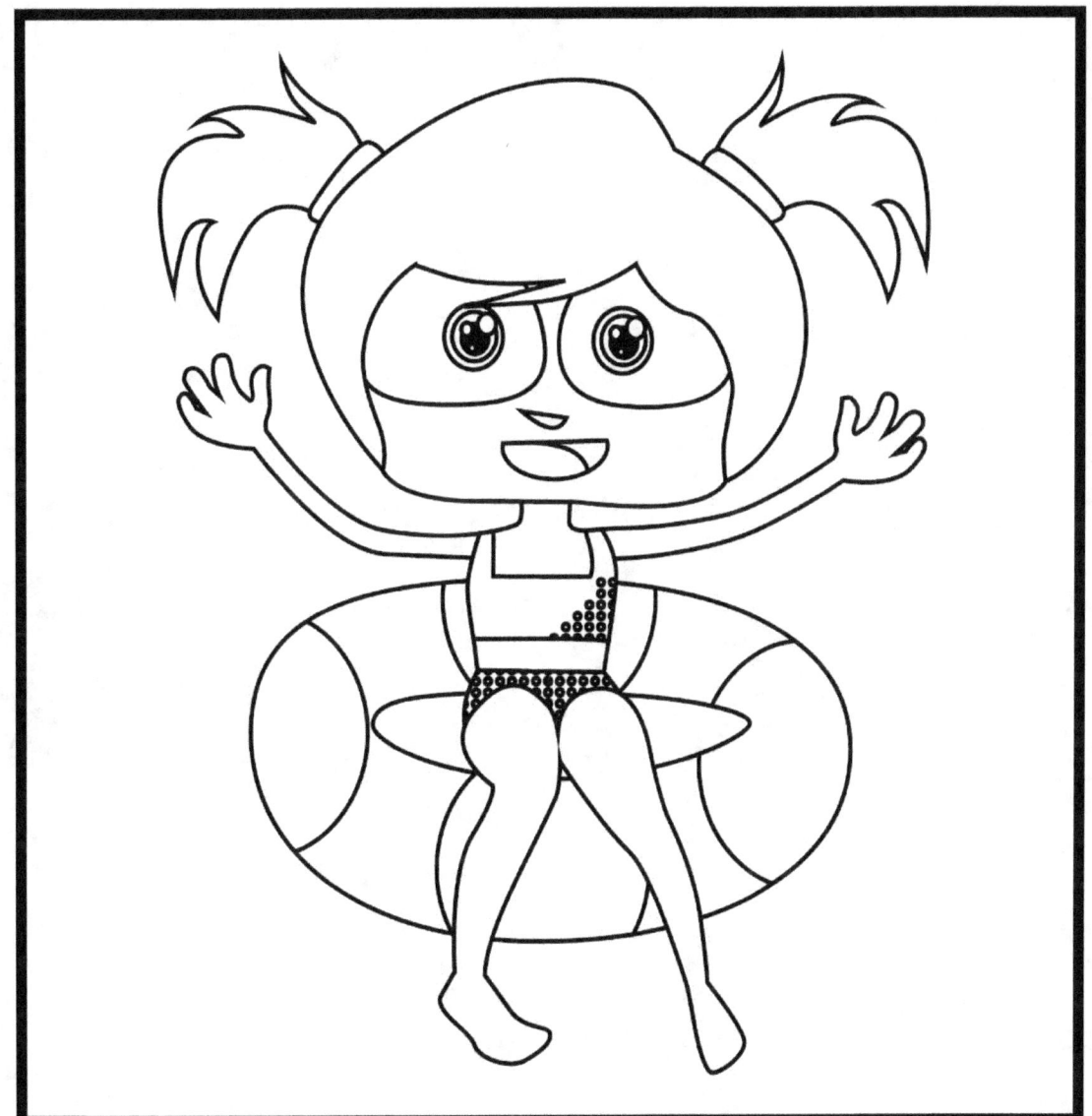

note:

_____

_____

_____

FEBRUARY 13TH

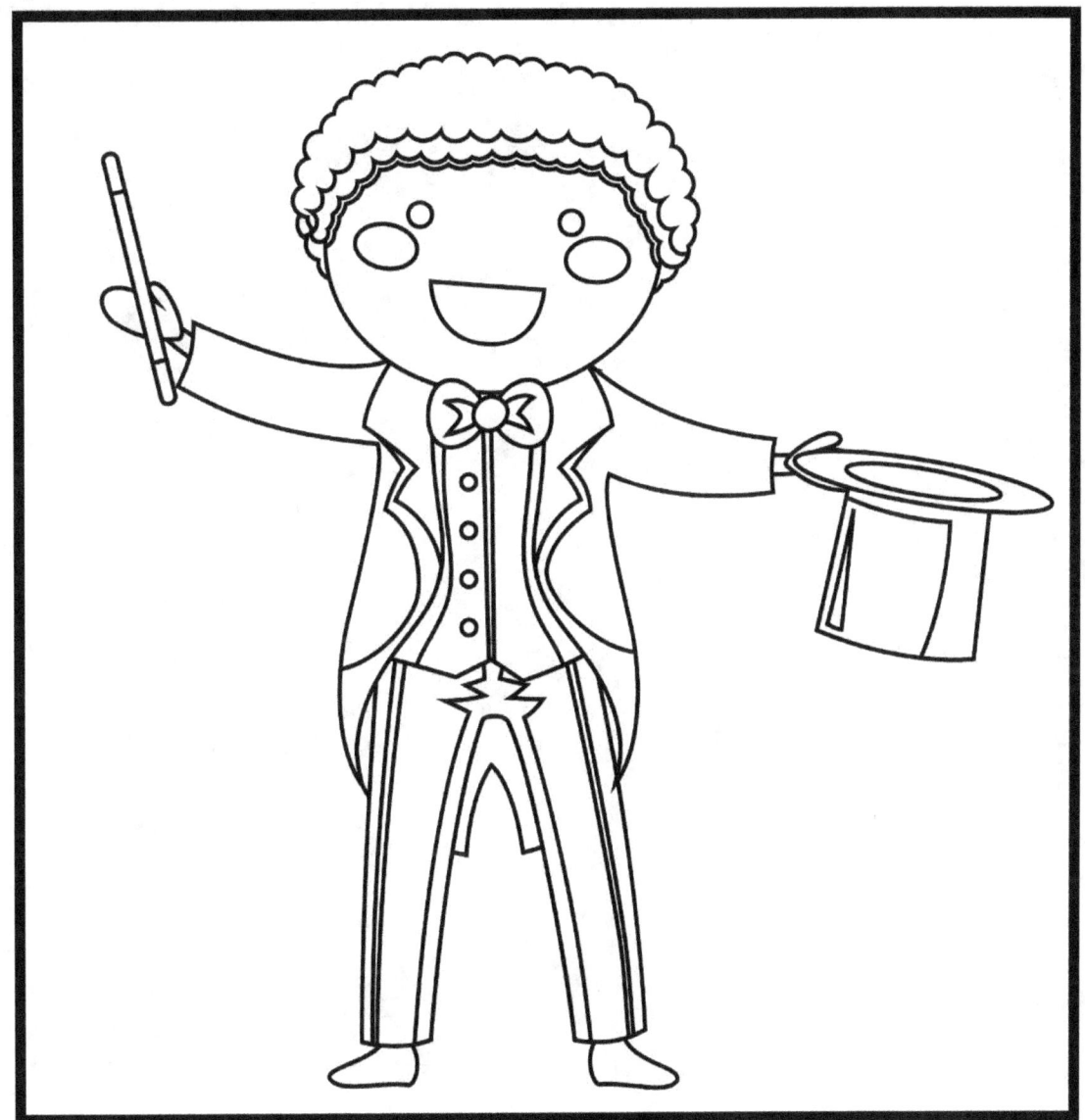

note:

_____

_____

_____

FEBRUARY 14TH

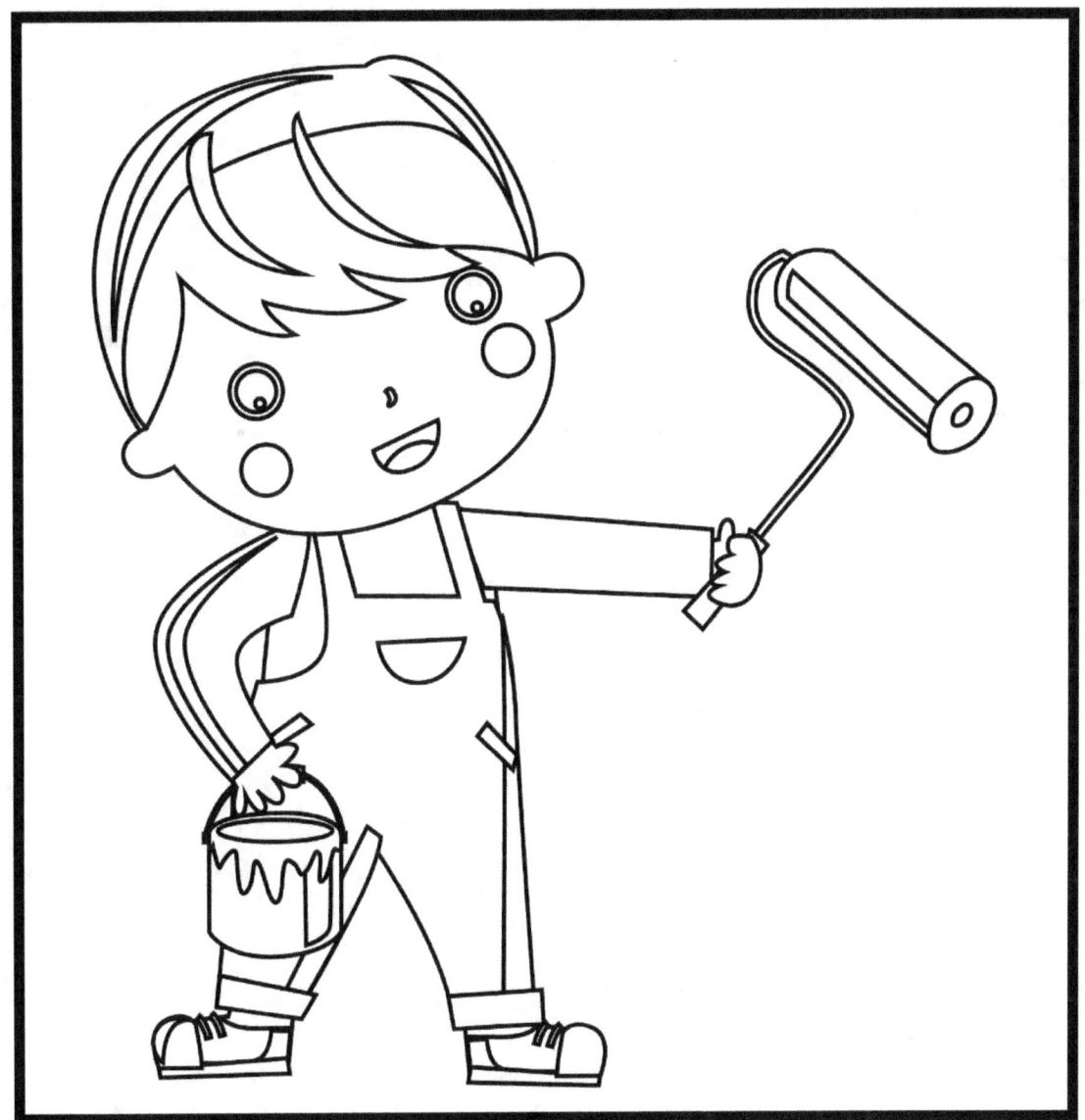

note:

_____

_____

_____

FEBRUARY 14TH

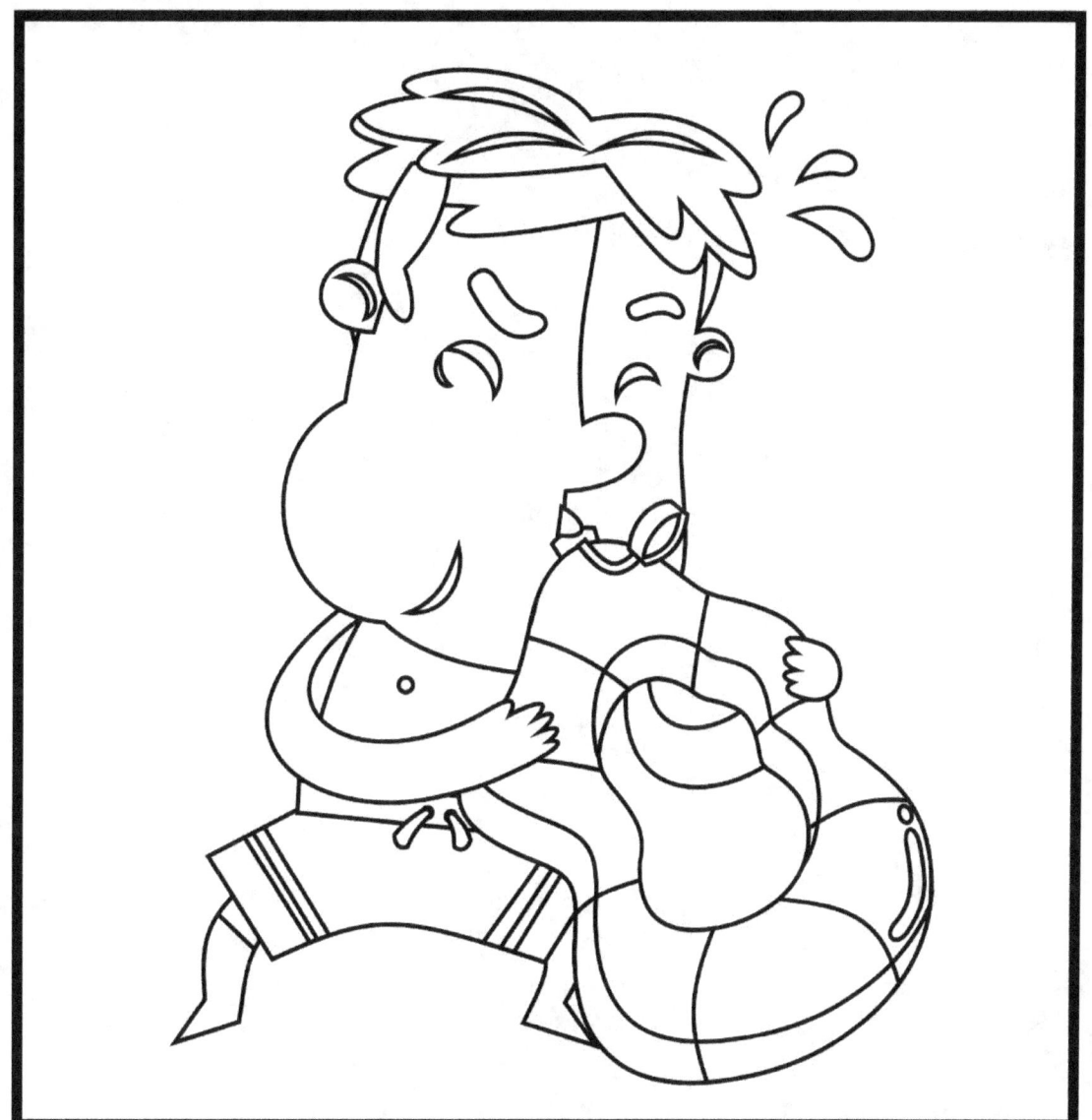

note:

_____

_____

_____

FEBRUARY 16TH

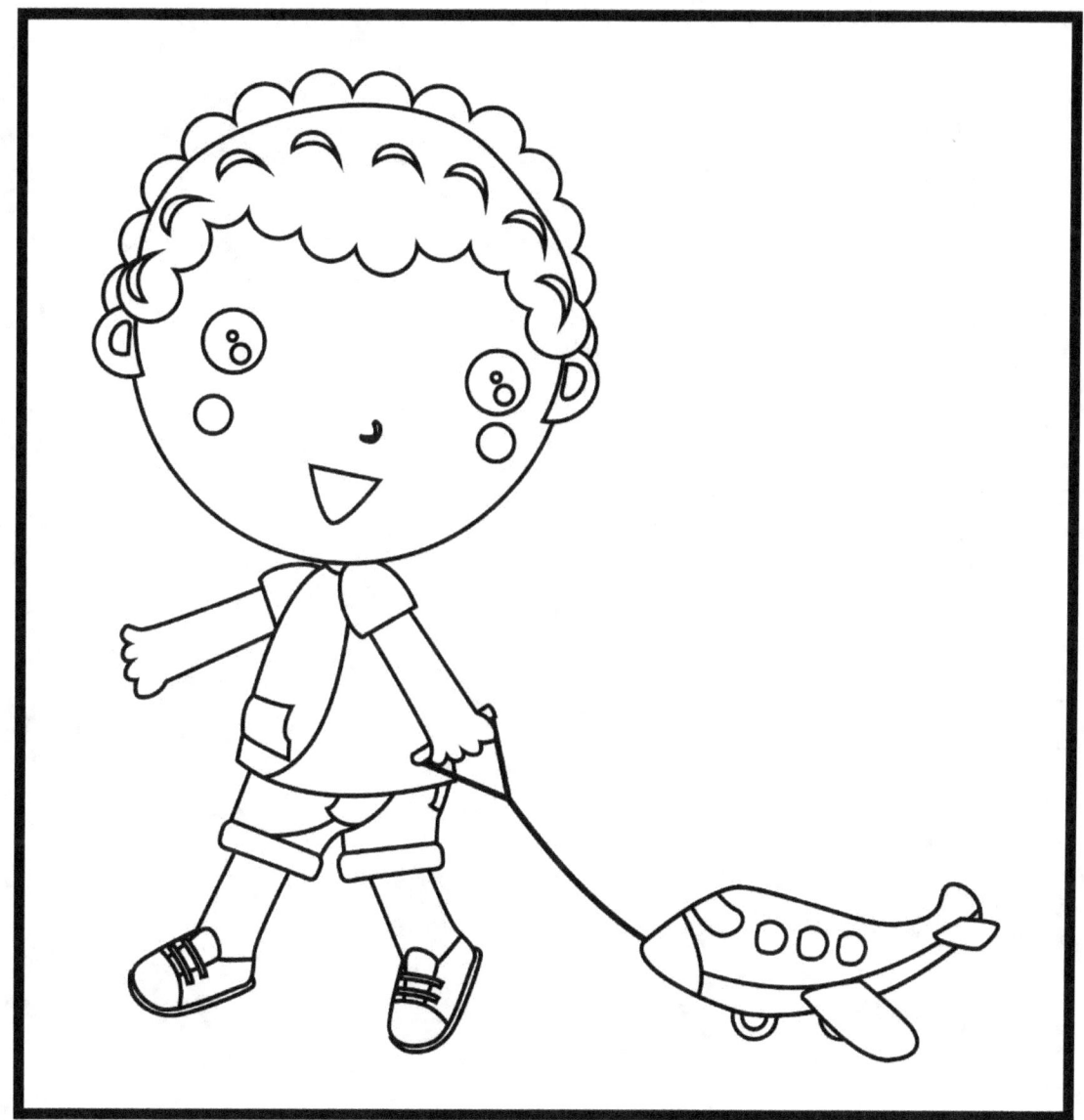

note:

_____

_____

_____

FEBRUARY 17TH

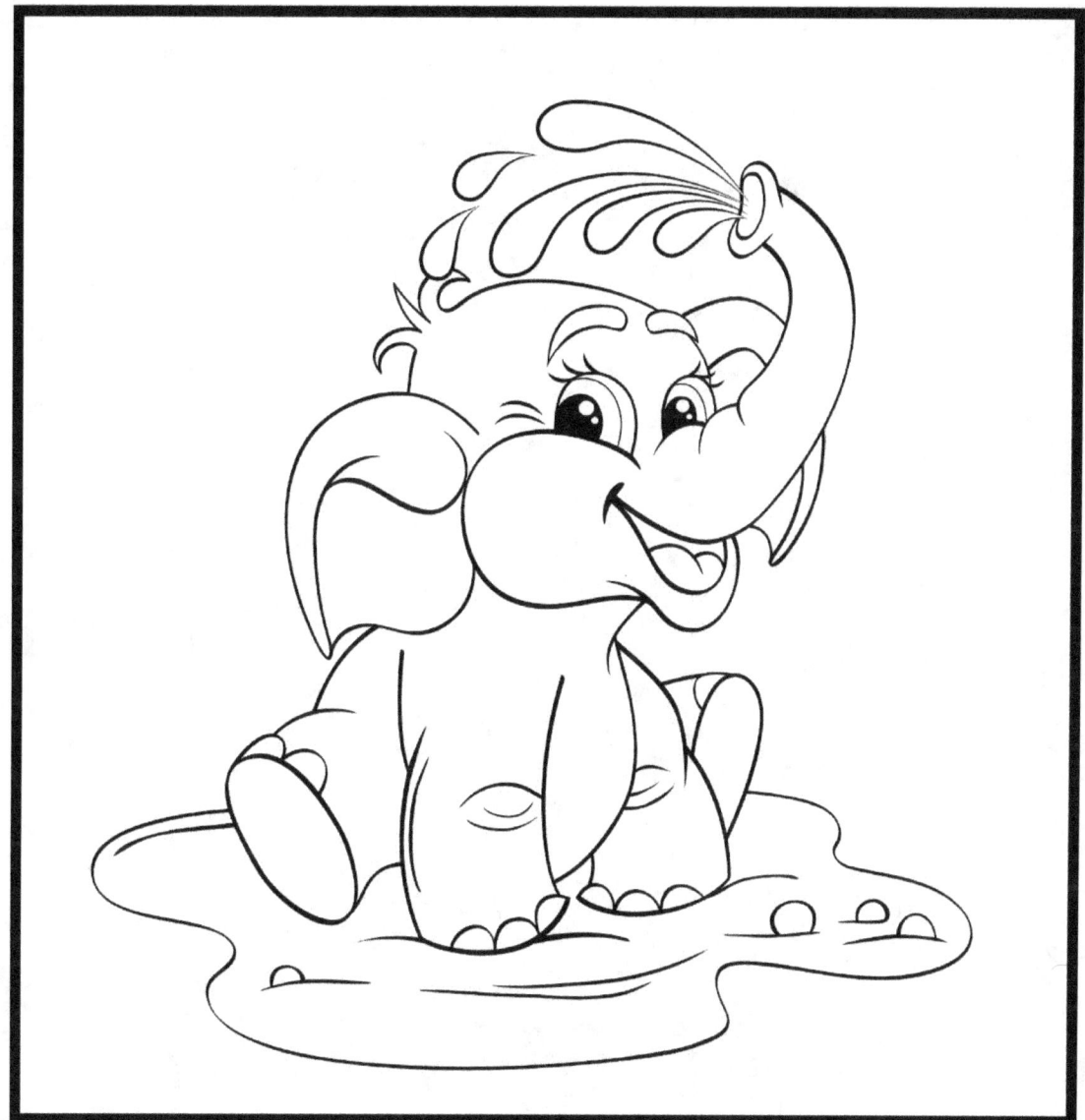

note:

_____

_____

_____

FEBRUARY 18TH

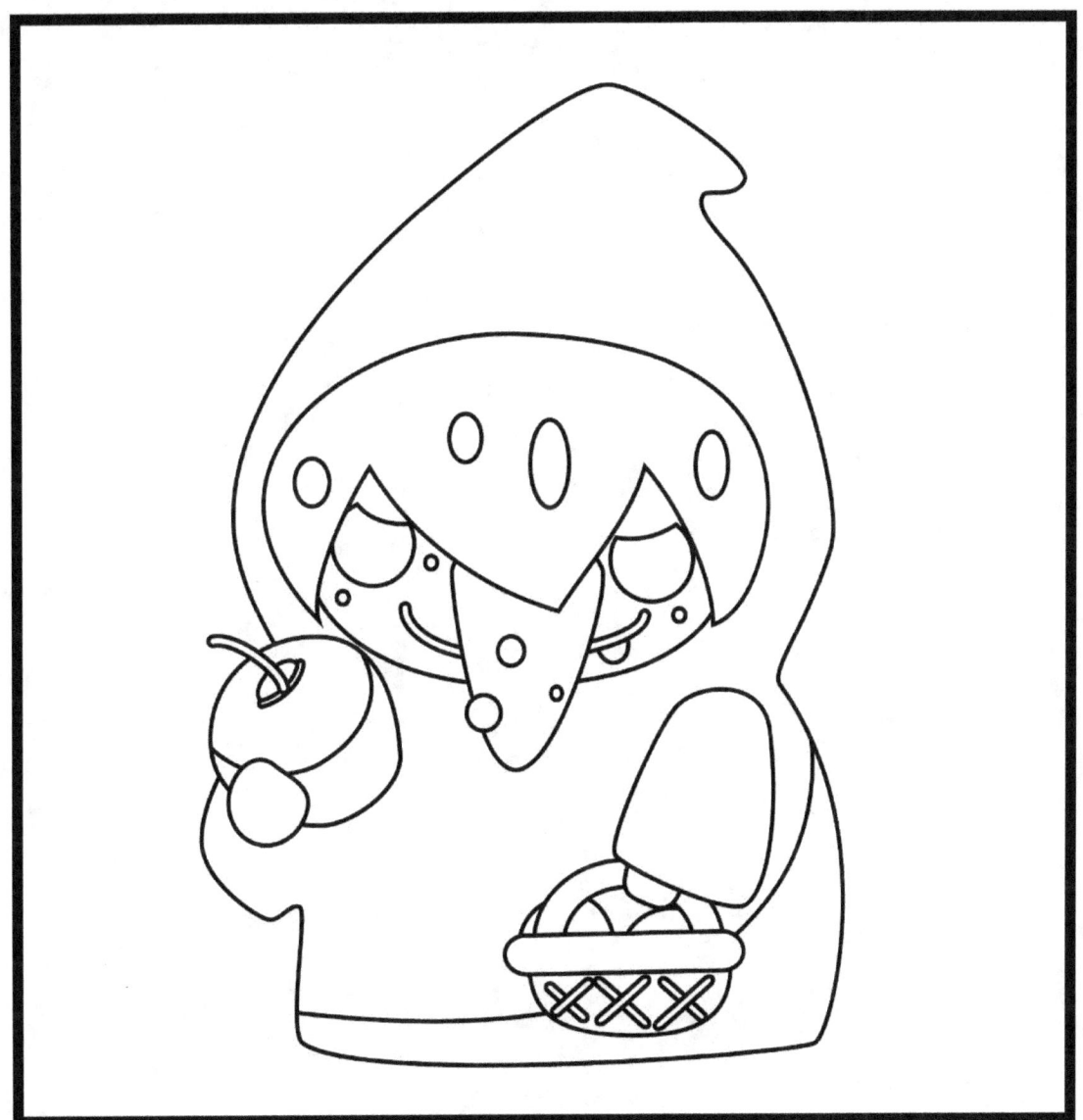

note:

_____

_____

_____

FEBRUARY 19TH

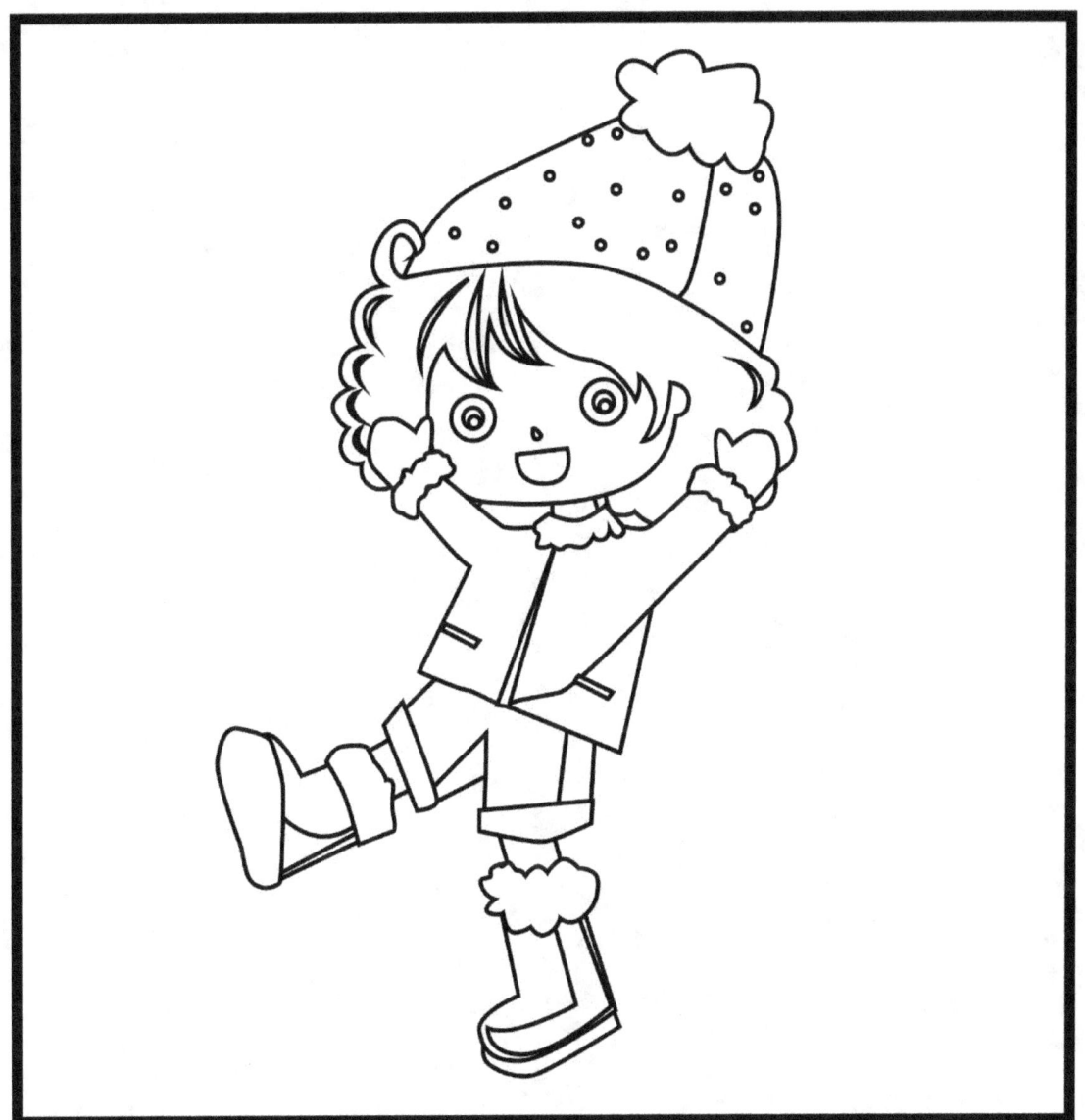

note:

_____

_____

_____

FEBRUARY 20TH

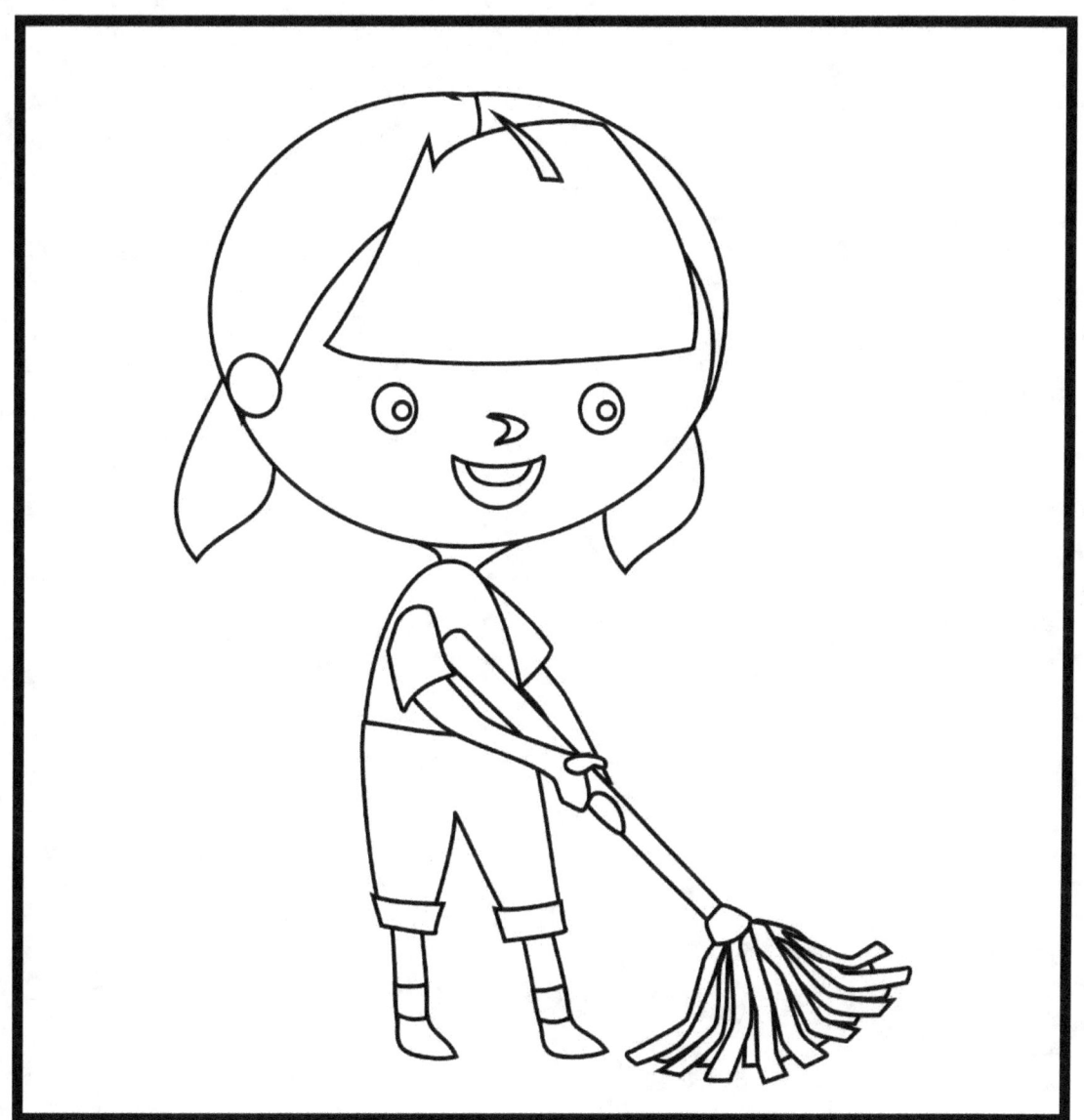

note:

_____

_____

_____

FEBRUARY 21TH

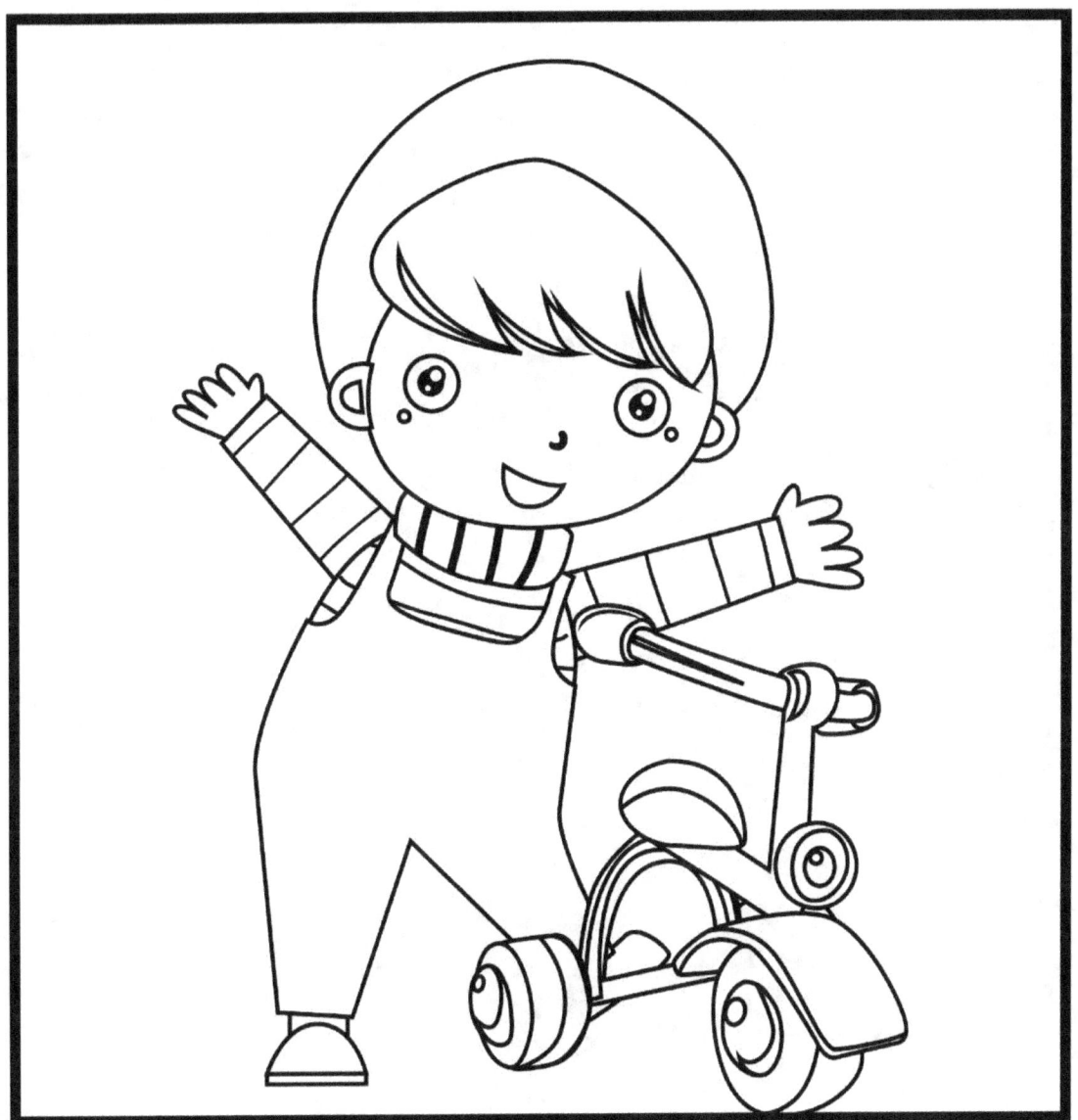

note:

_____

_____

_____

FEBRUARY 22TH

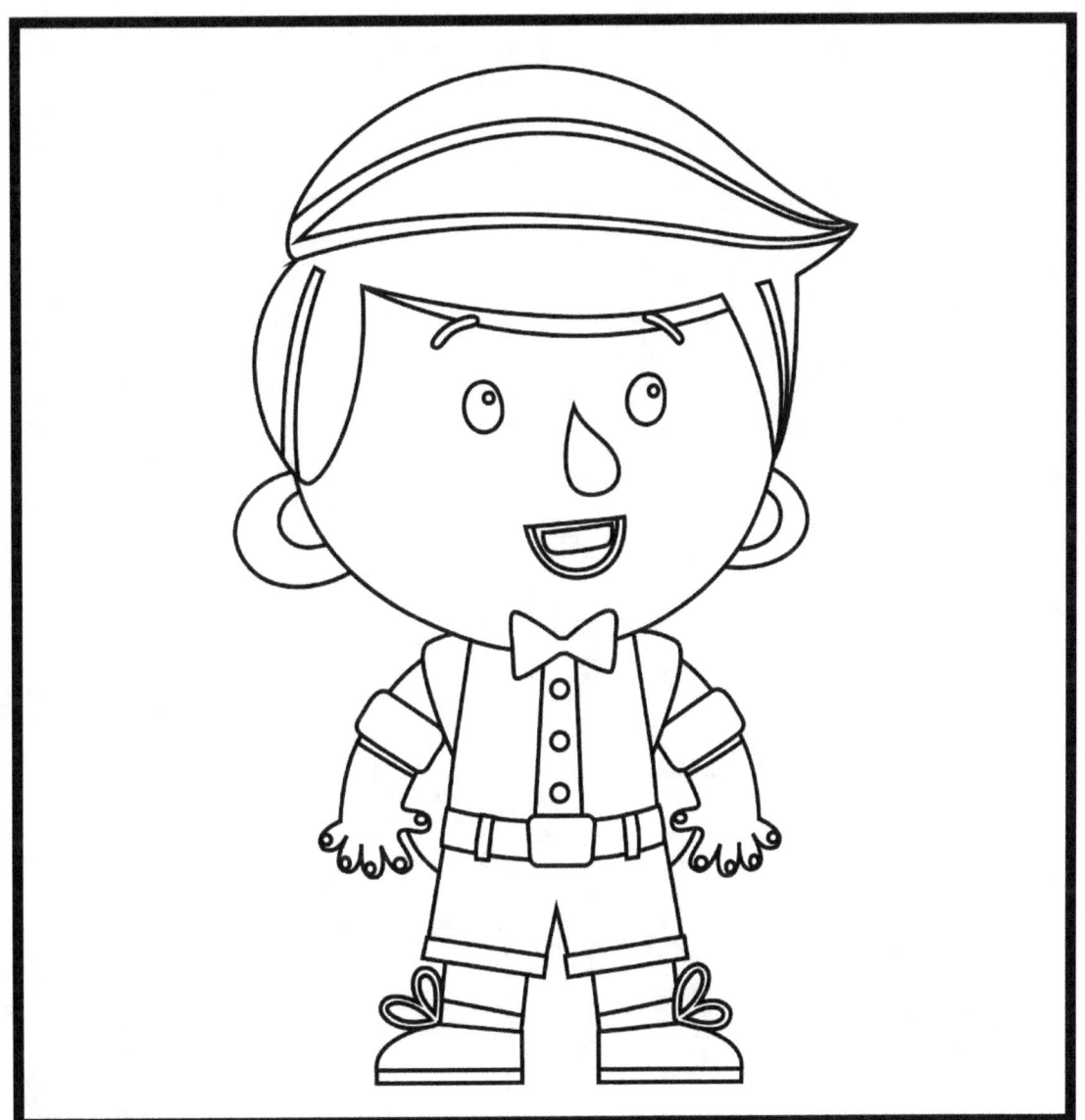

note:

_____

_____

_____

FEBRUARY 23TH

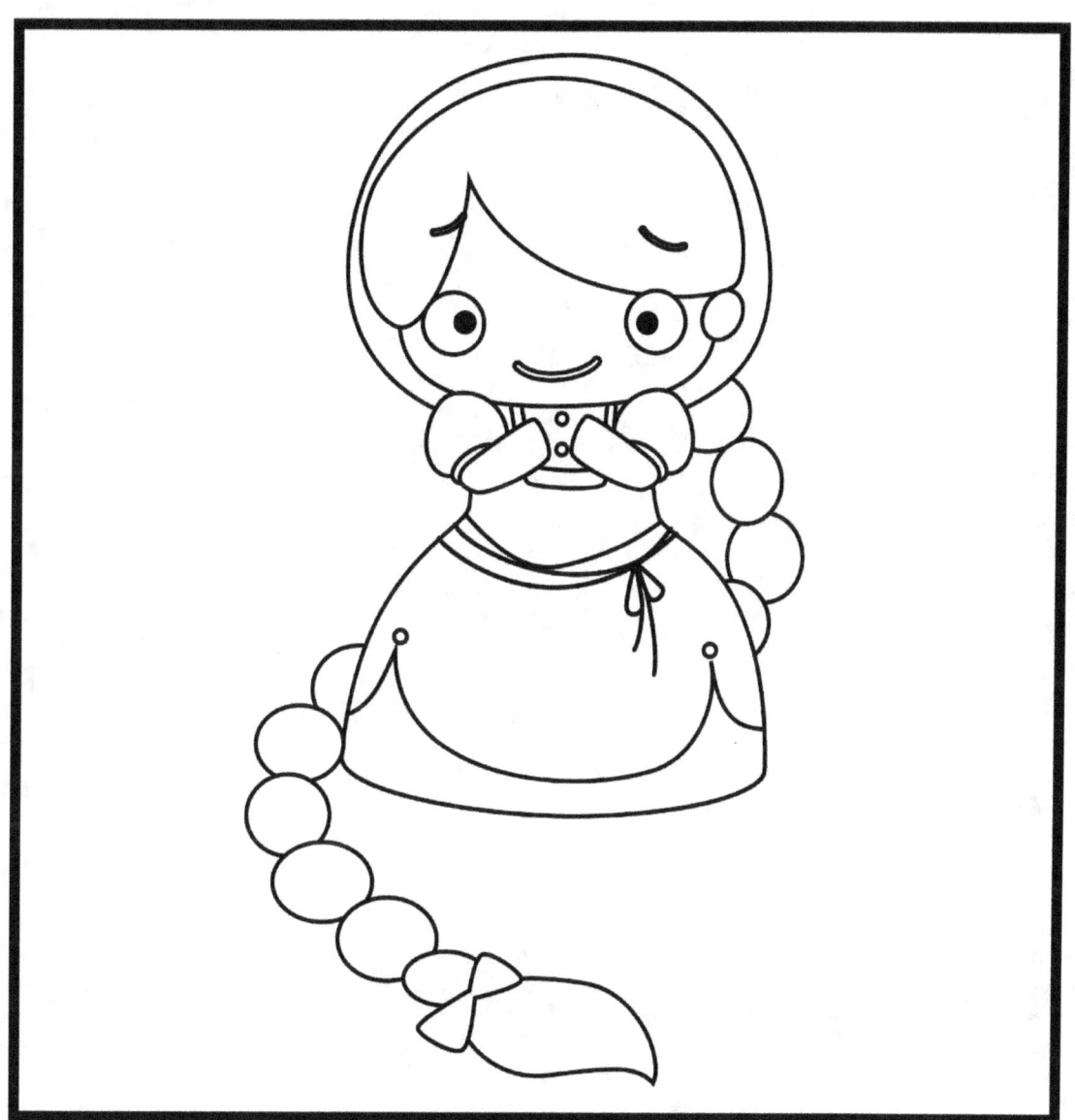

note:

_____

_____

_____

FEBRUARY 24TH

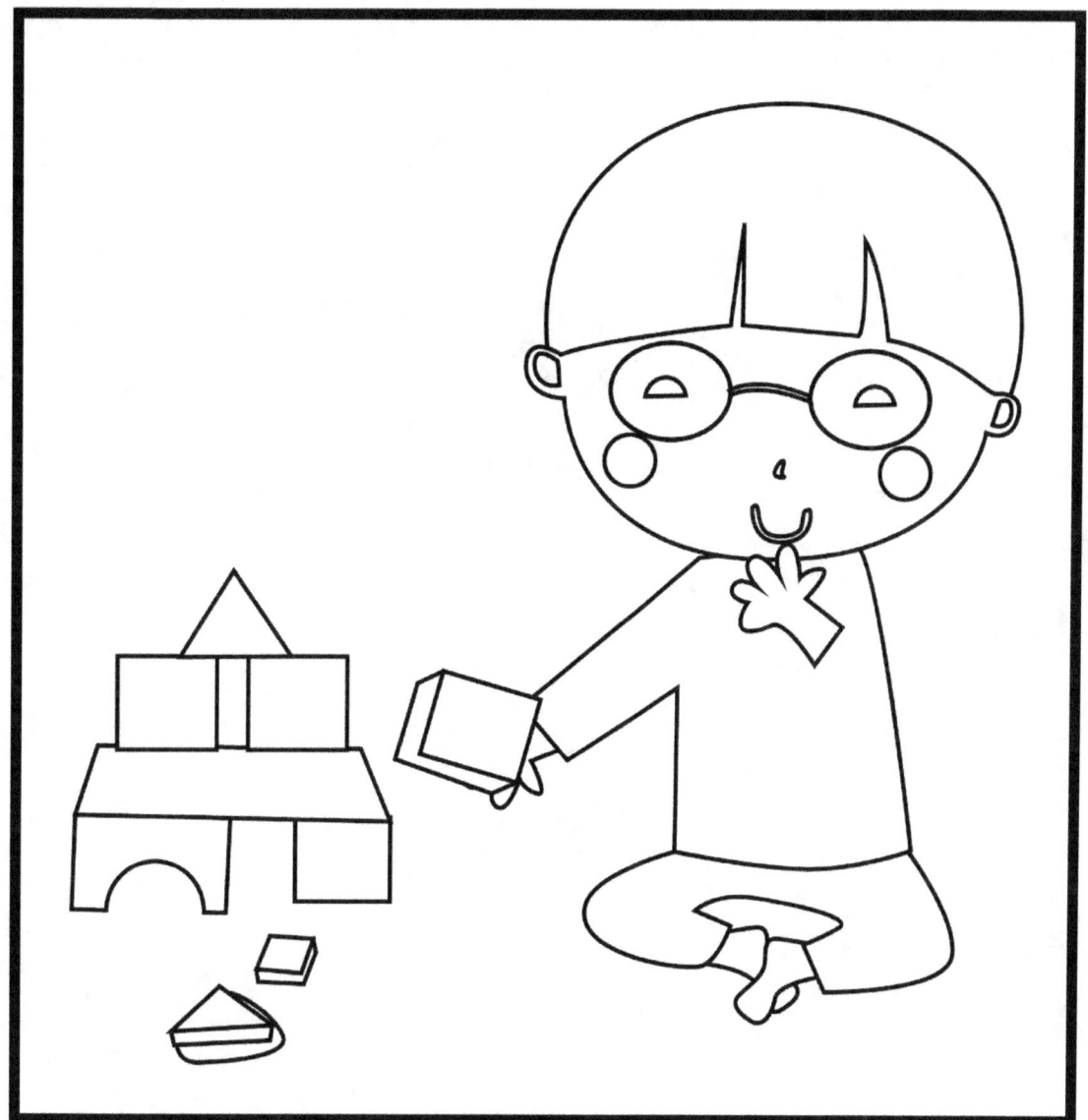

note:

_____

_____

_____

FEBRUARY 25TH

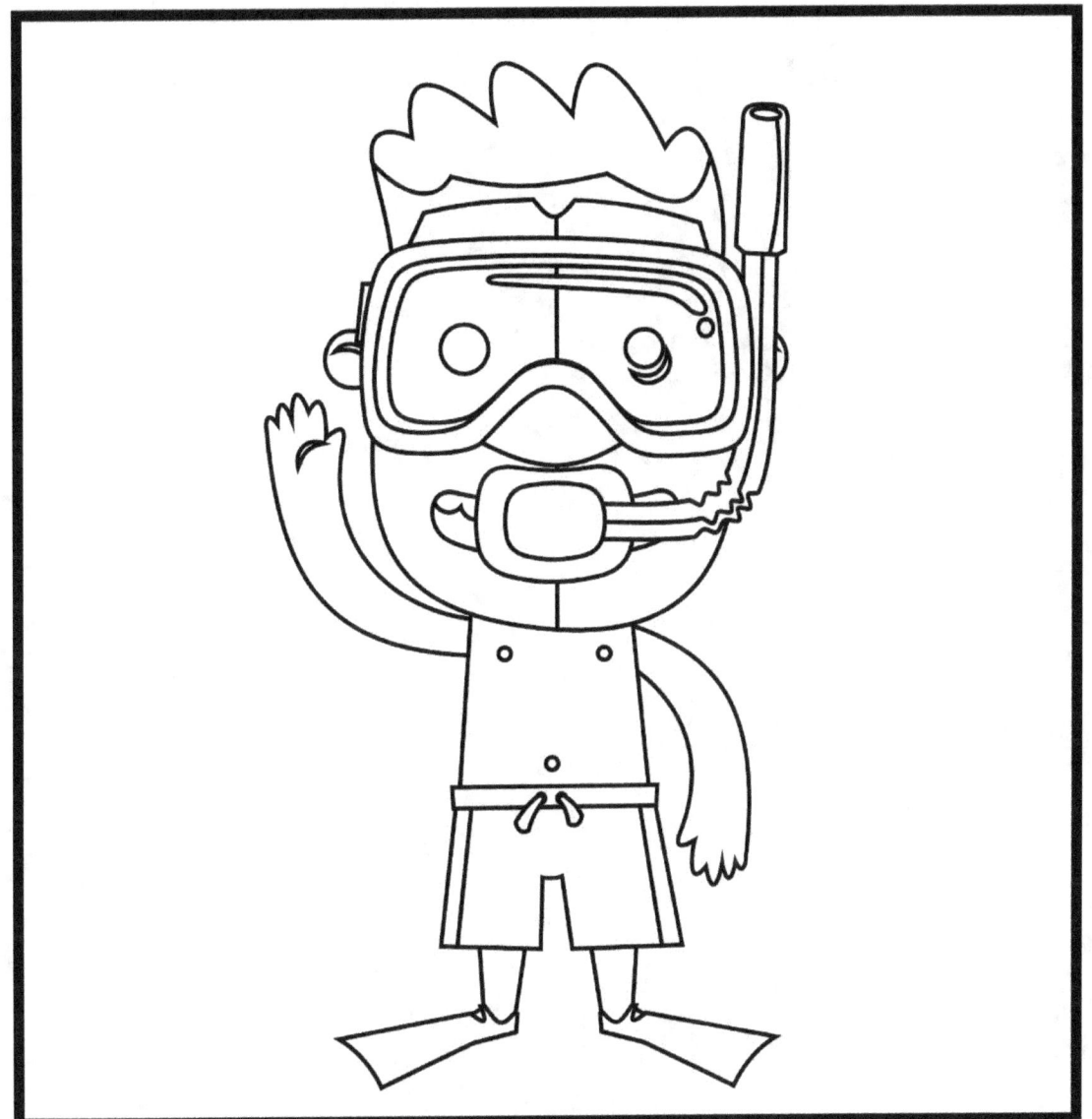

note:

_____

_____

_____

FEBRUARY 26TH

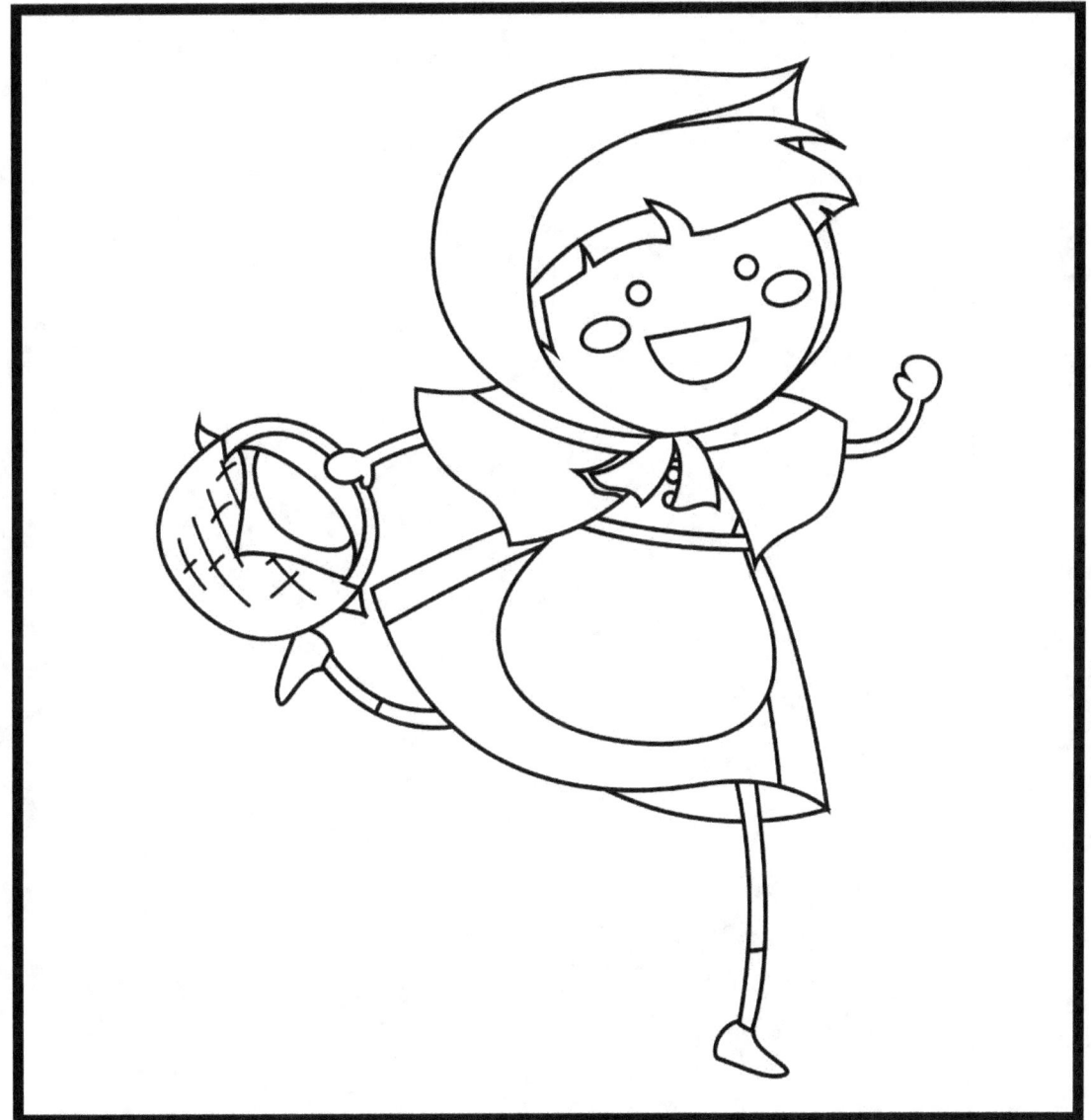

note:

_____

_____

_____

FEBRUARY 27TH

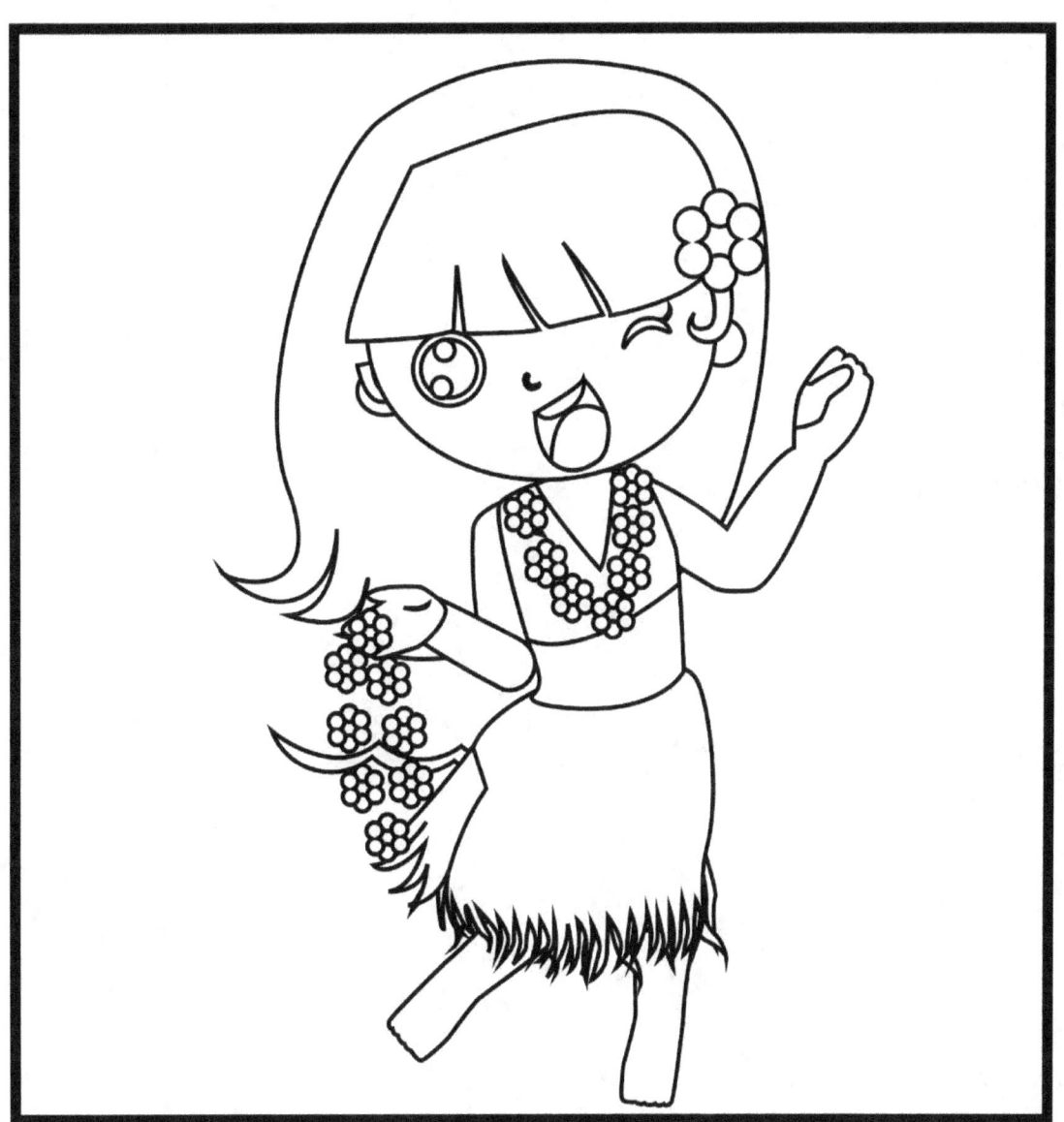

note:

_____

_____

_____

FEBRUARY 28TH

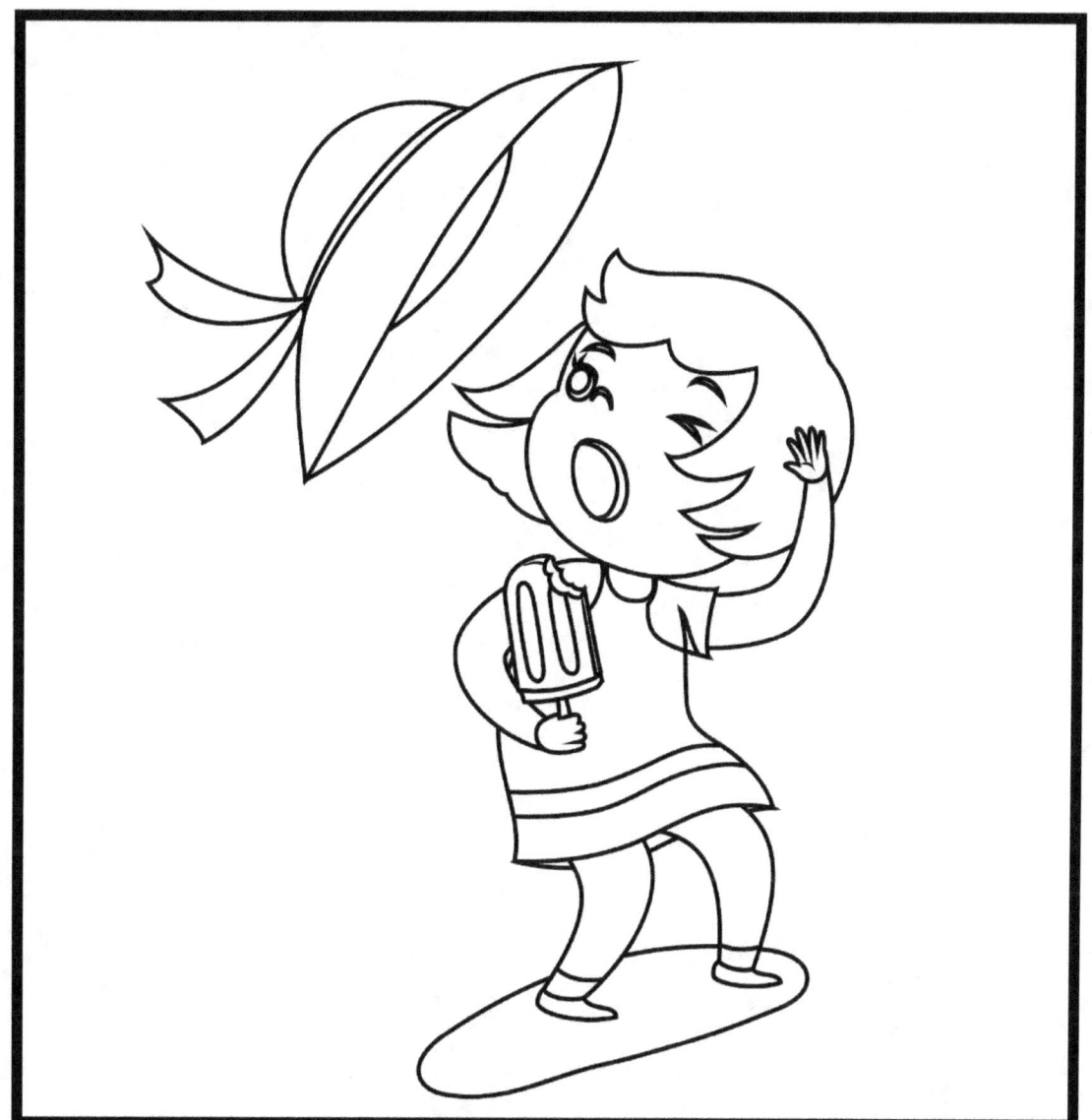

note:

_____

_____

_____

FEBRUARY 29TH

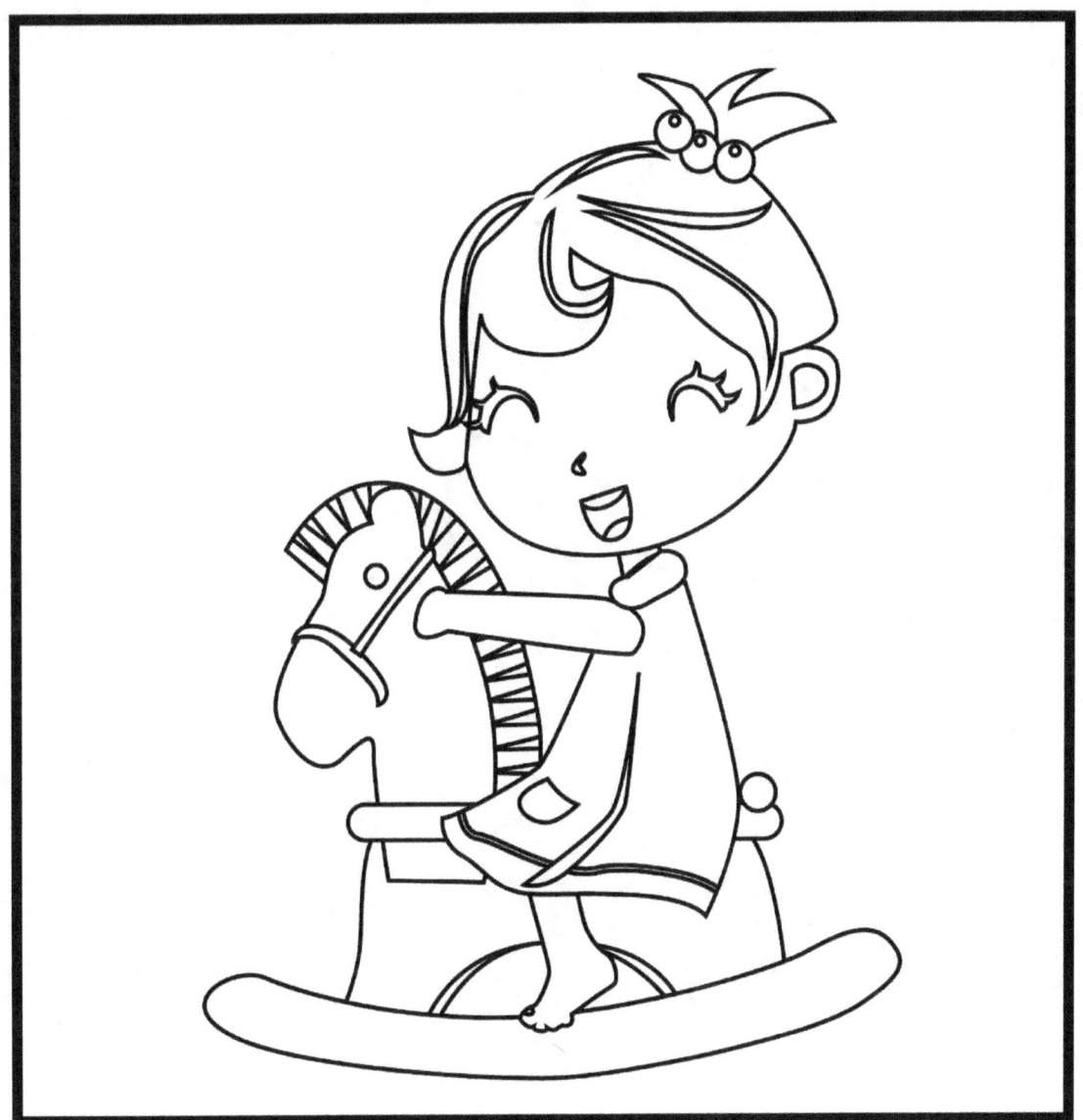

note:

_____

_____

_____

FEBRUARY 30TH

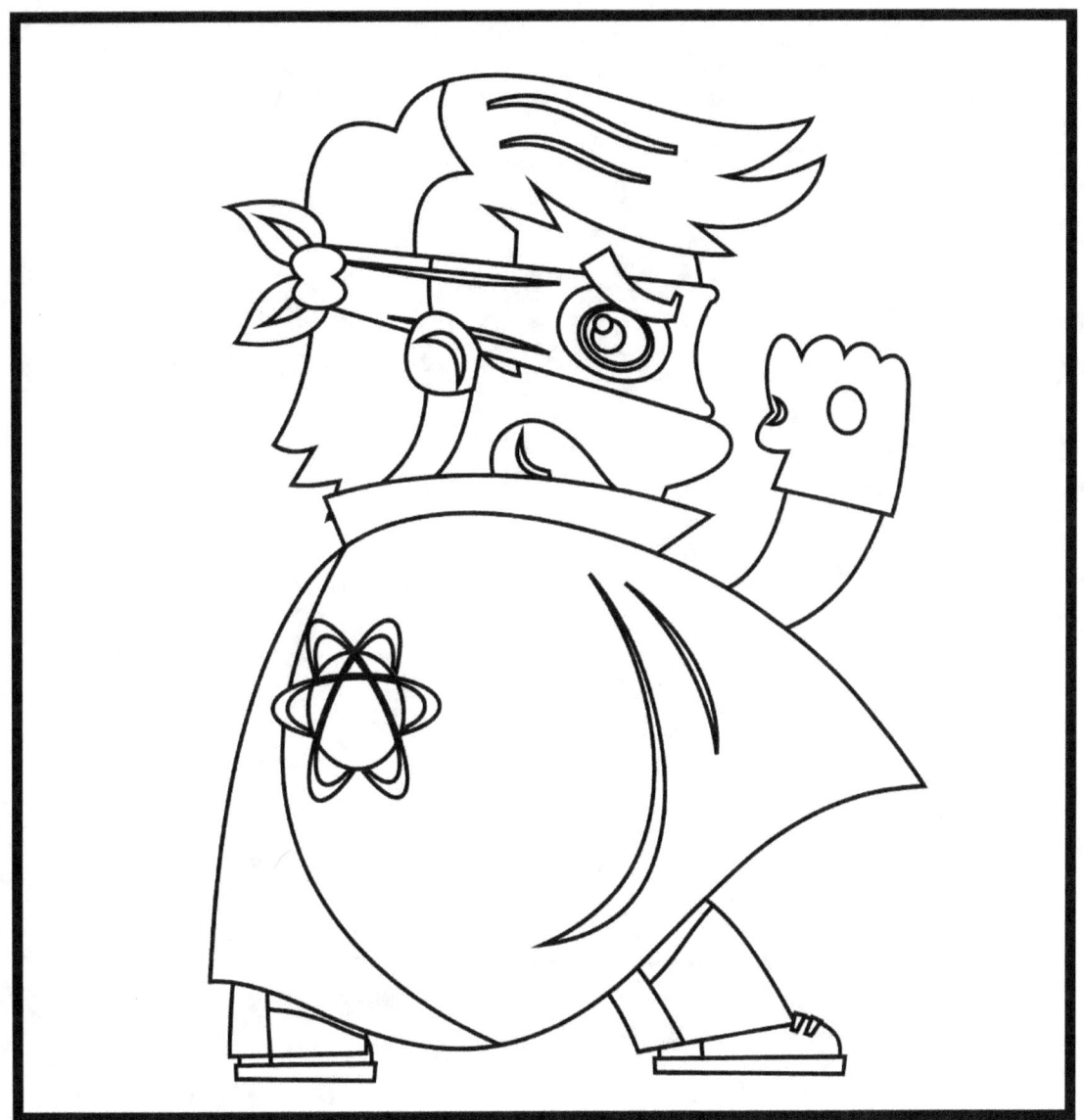

note:

_____

_____

_____

FEBRUARY 31TH

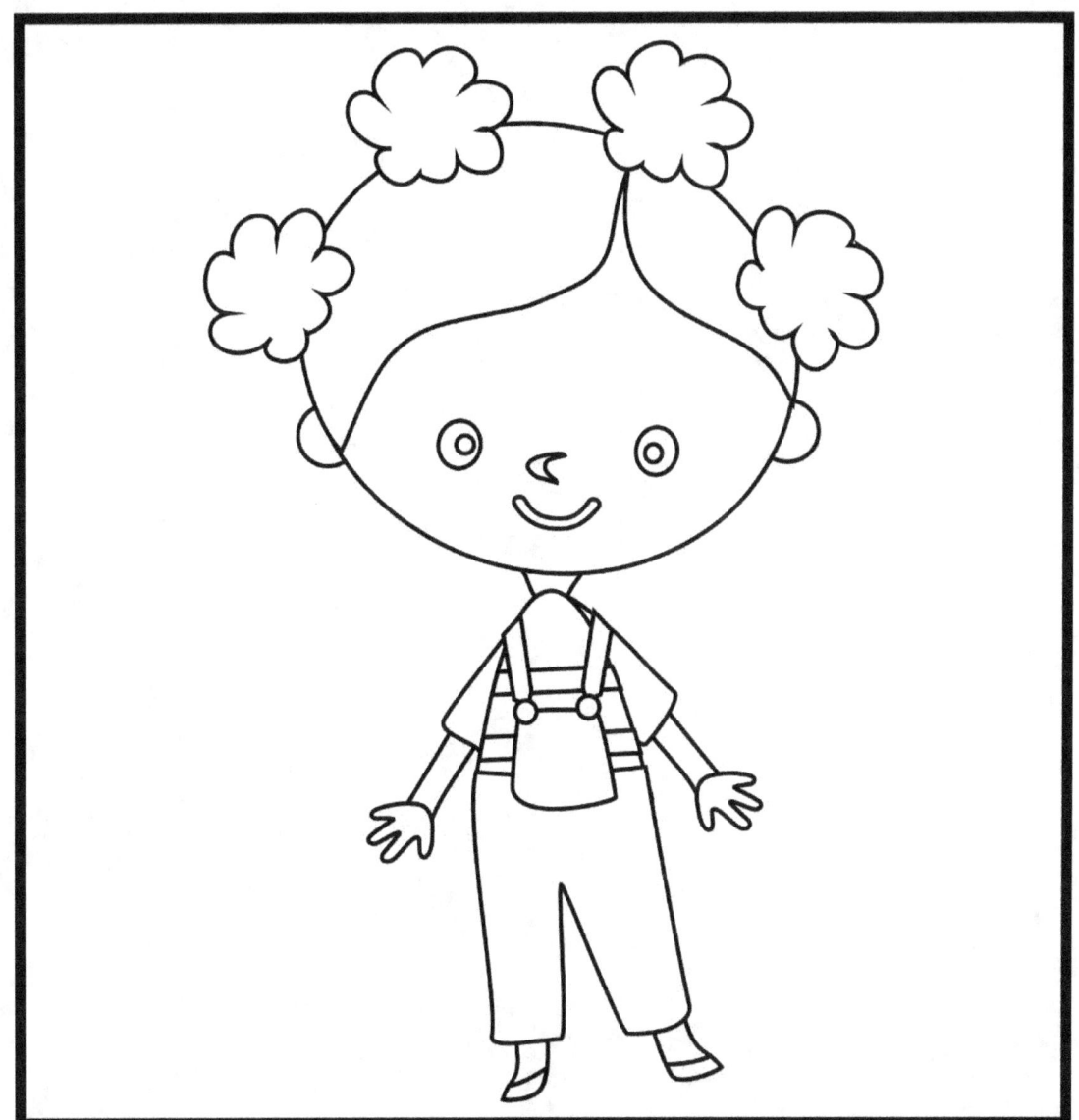

note:

_____

_____

_____

FEBRUARY 32TH

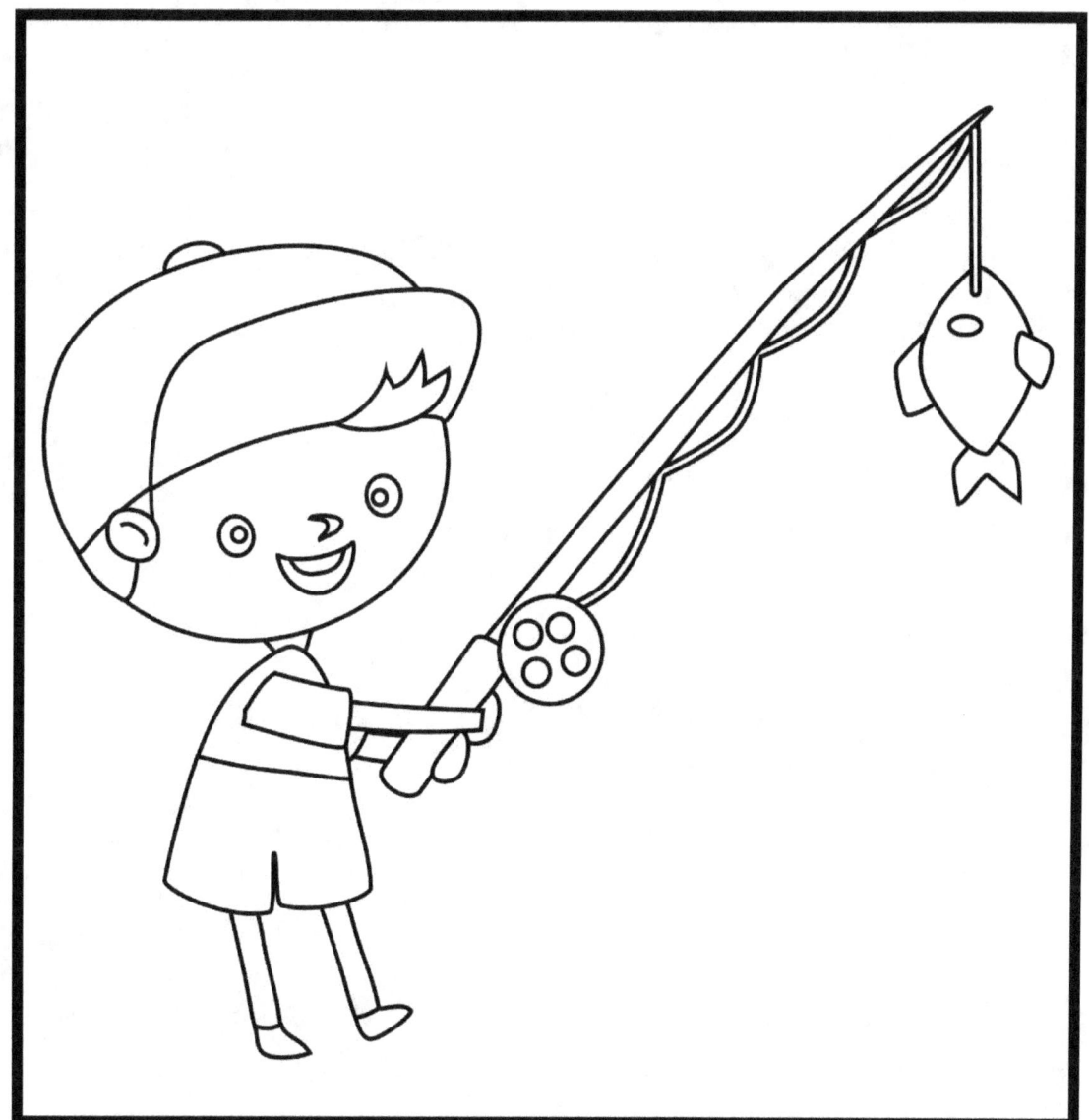

note:

_____

_____

_____

FEBRUARY 33TH

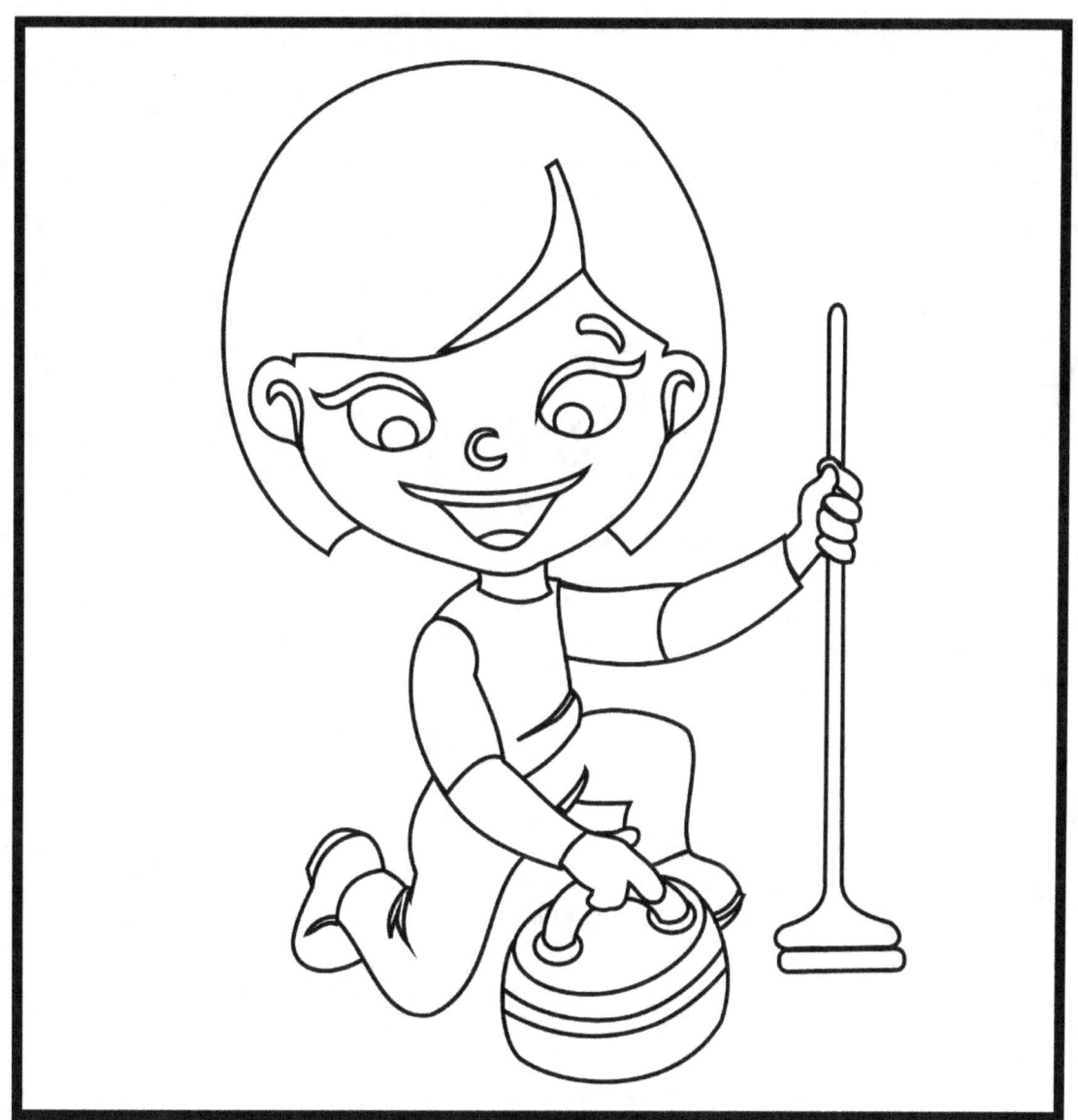

note:

_____

_____

_____

FEBRUARY 34TH

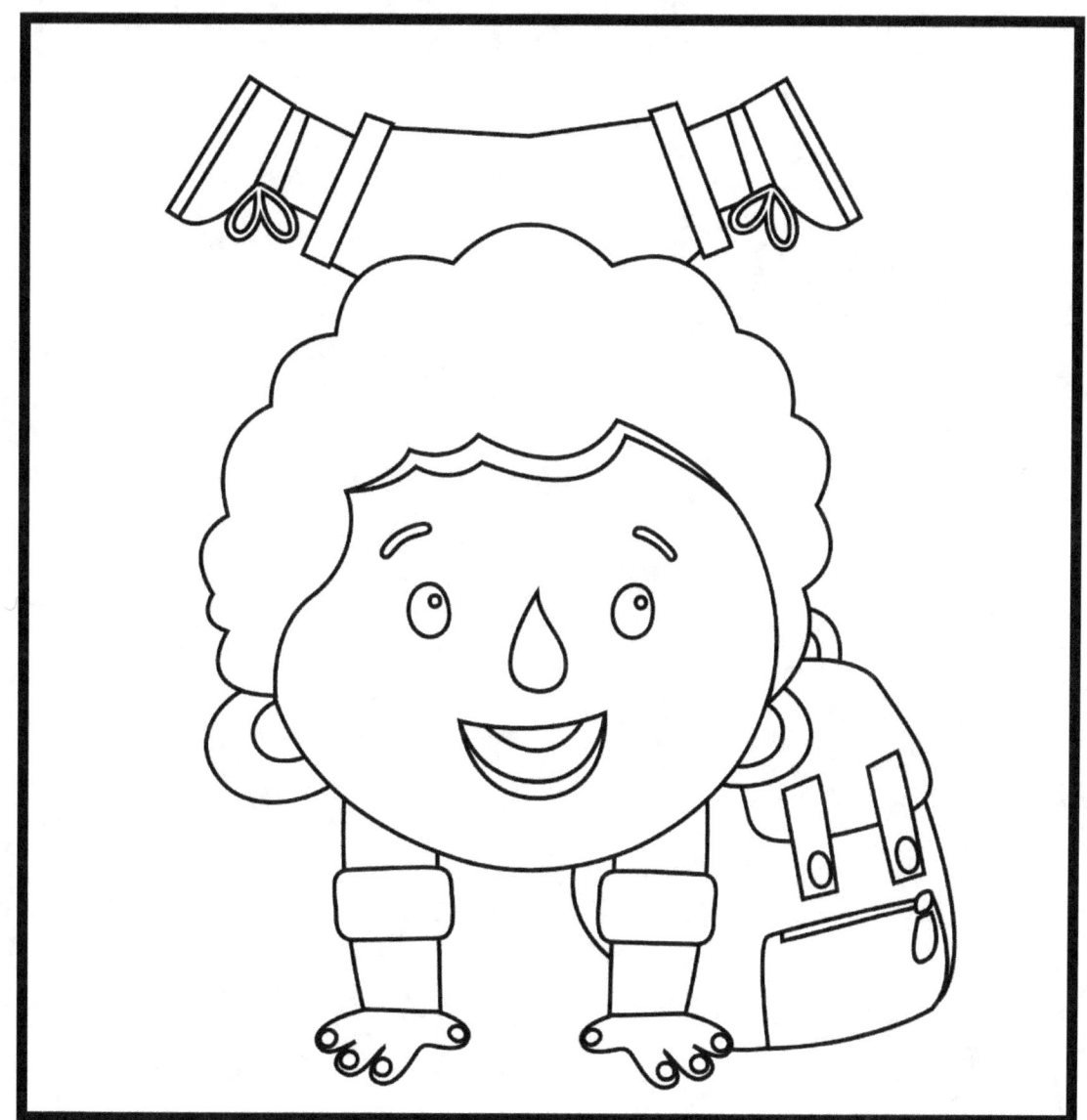

note:

_____

_____

_____

FEBRUARY 35TH

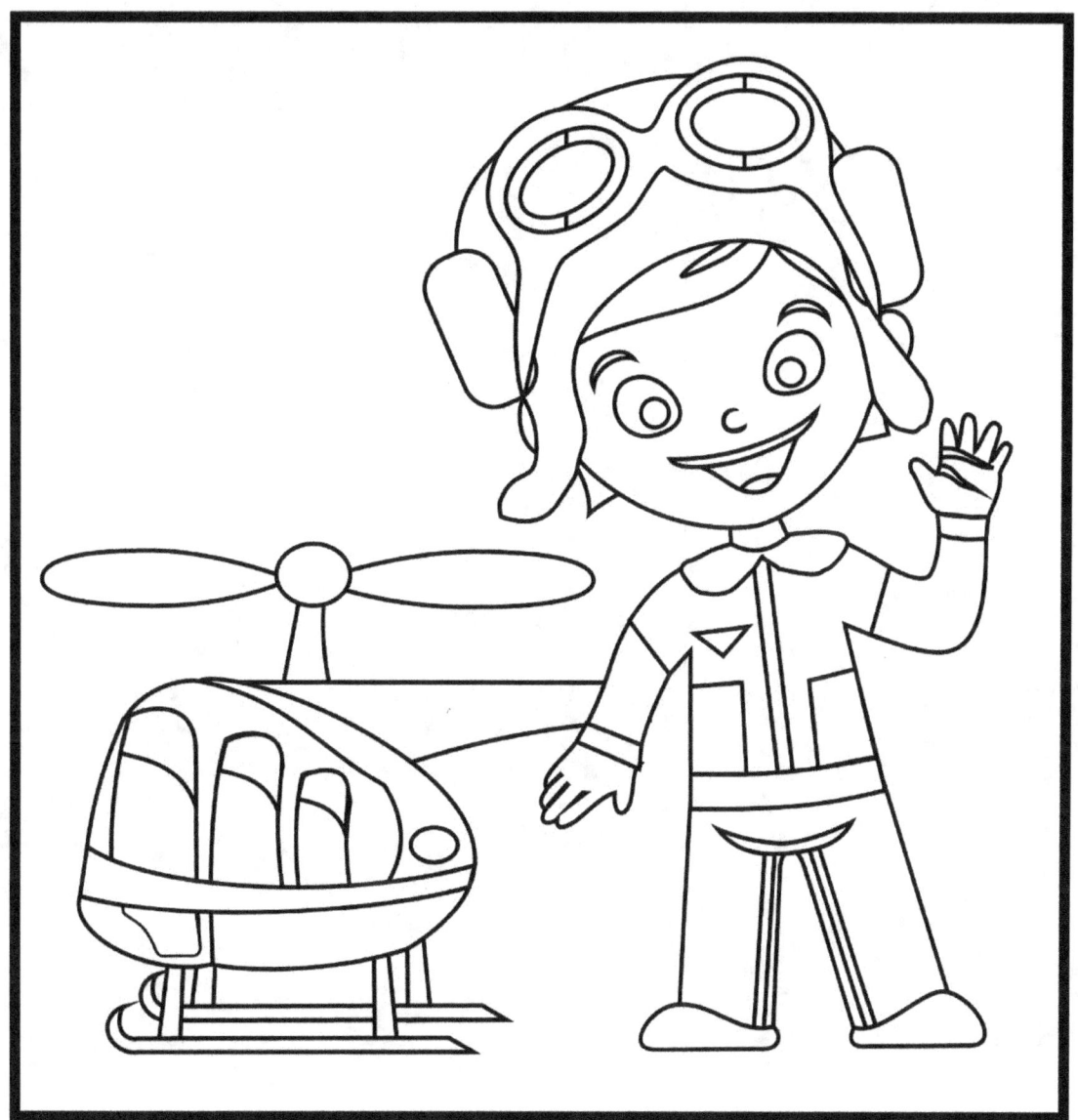

note:
_____
_____
_____

FEBRUARY 36TH

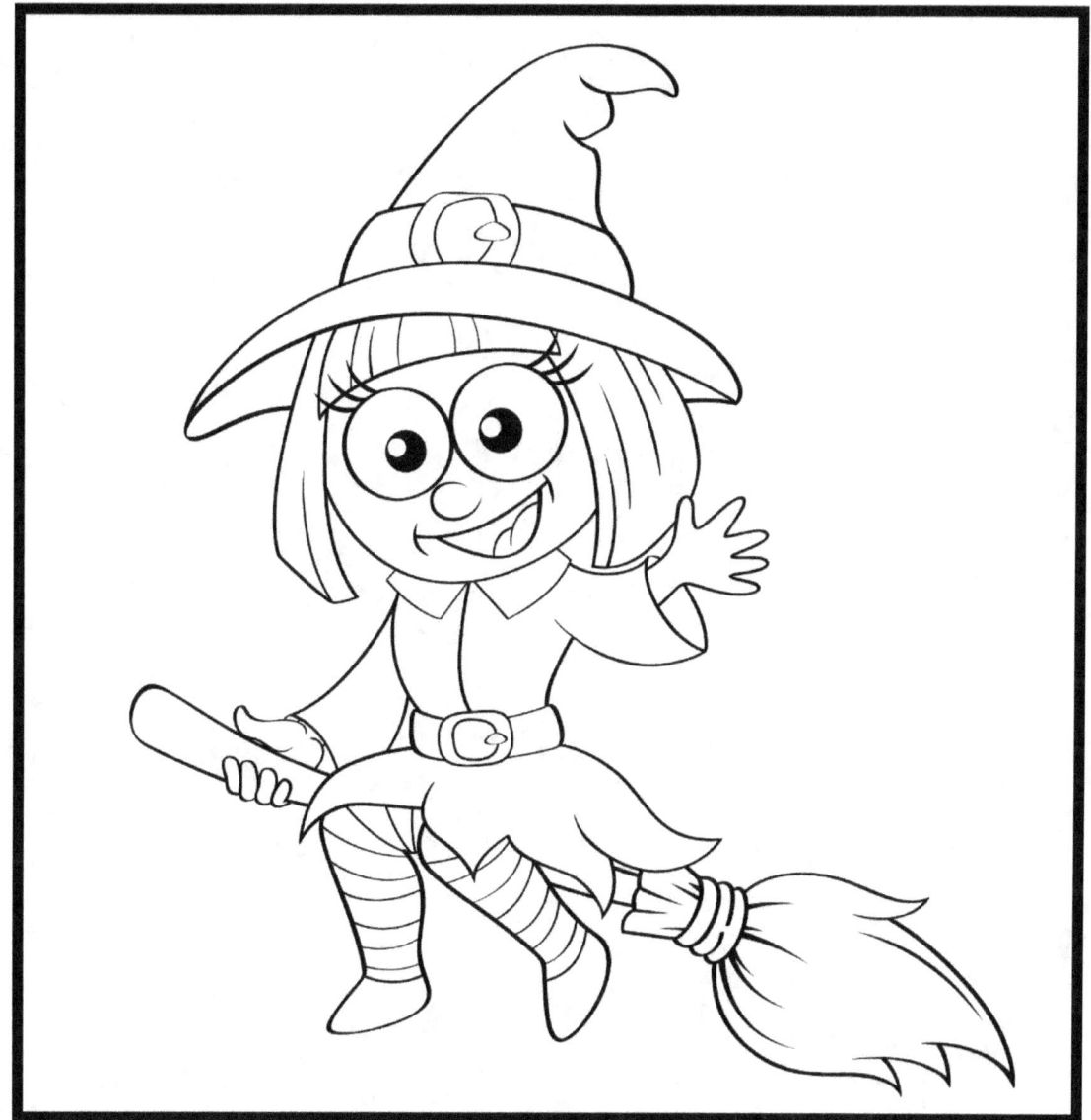

note:

_____

_____

_____

FEBRUARY 37TH

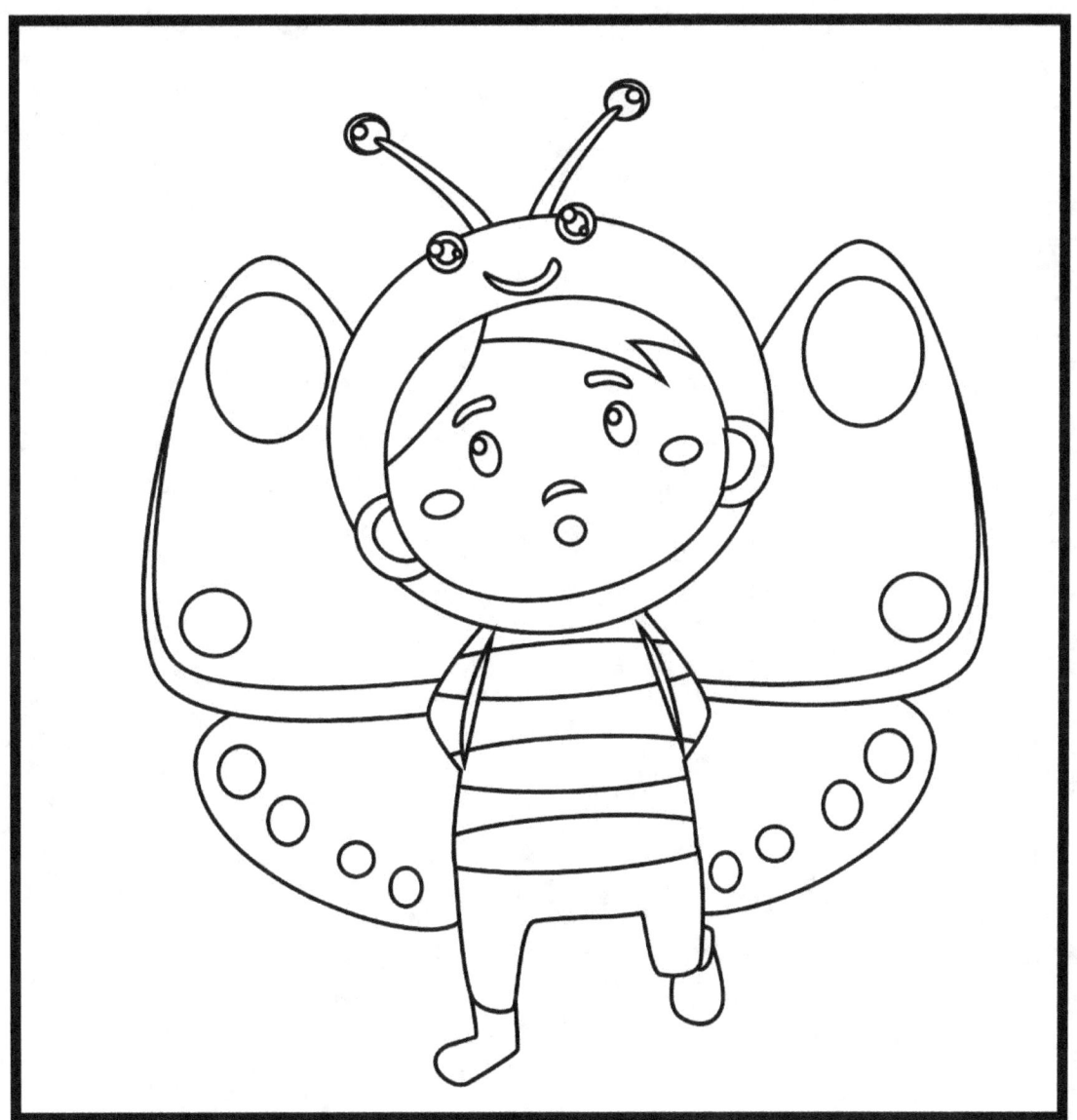

note:

_____

_____

_____

FEBRUARY 38TH

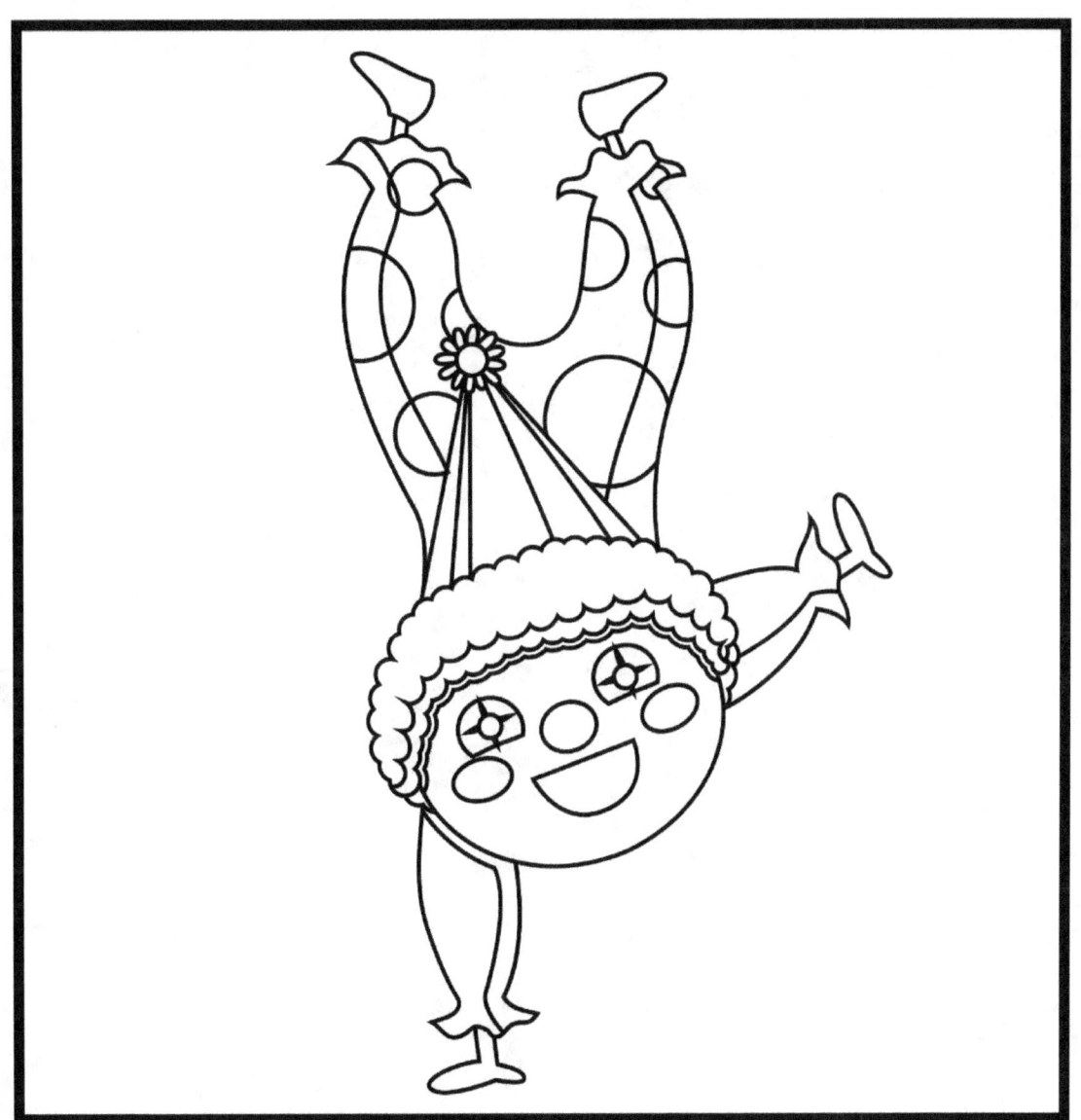

note:

_____

_____

_____

FEBRUARY 39TH

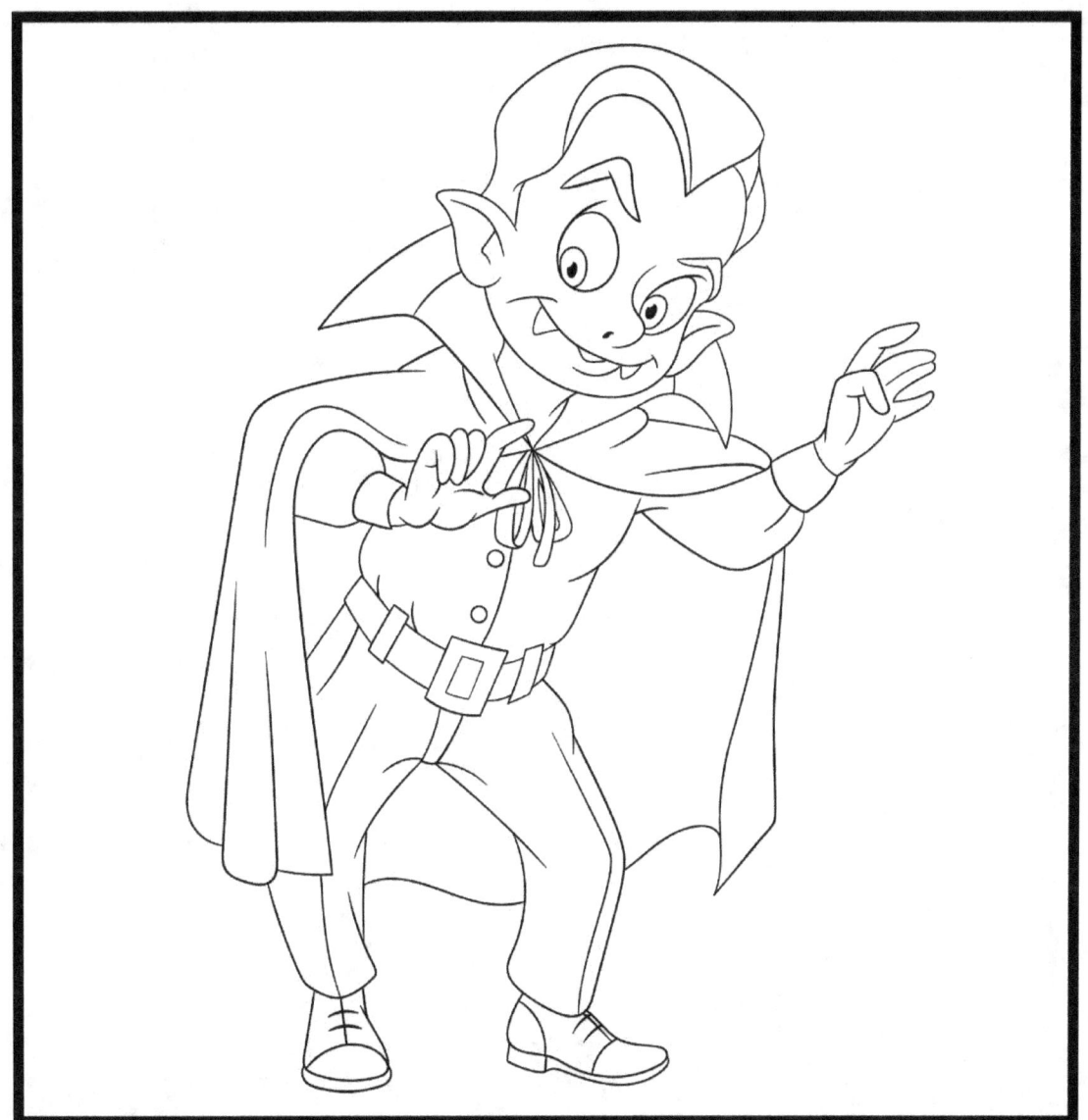

note:

_____

_____

_____

FEBRUARY 40TH

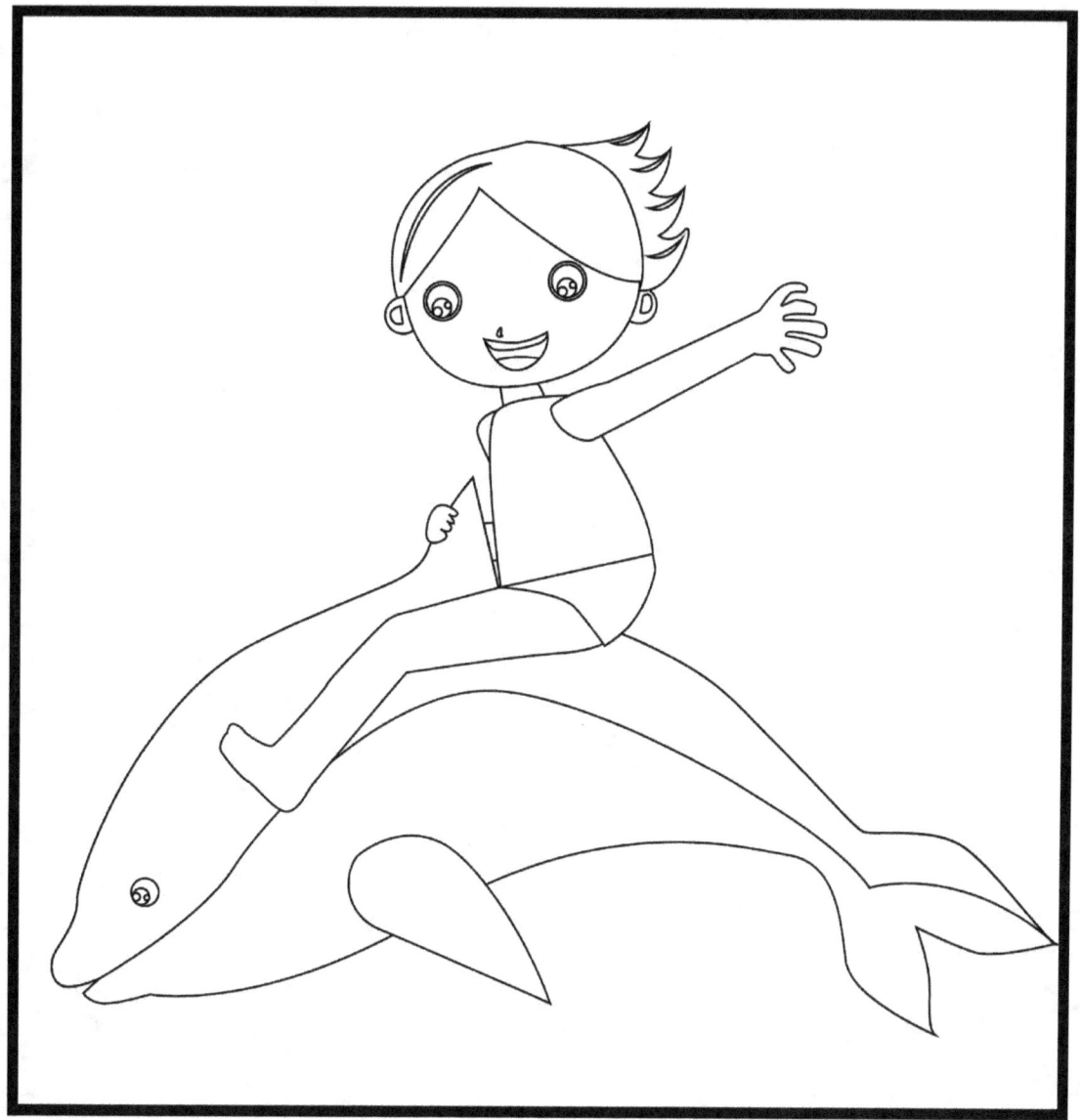

note:

_____

_____

_____

FEBRUARY 4TH

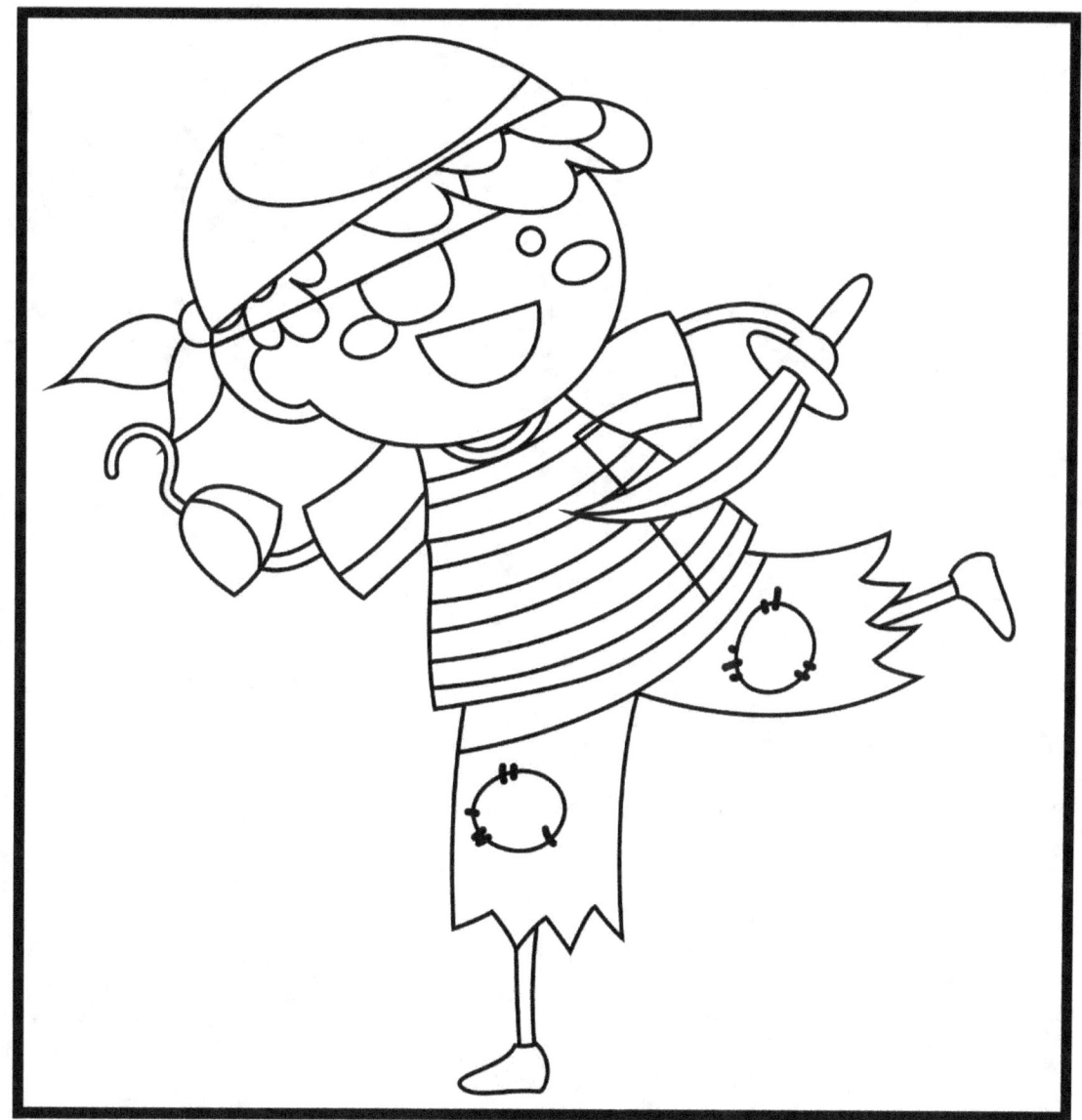

note:

_____

_____

_____

FEBRUARY 42TH

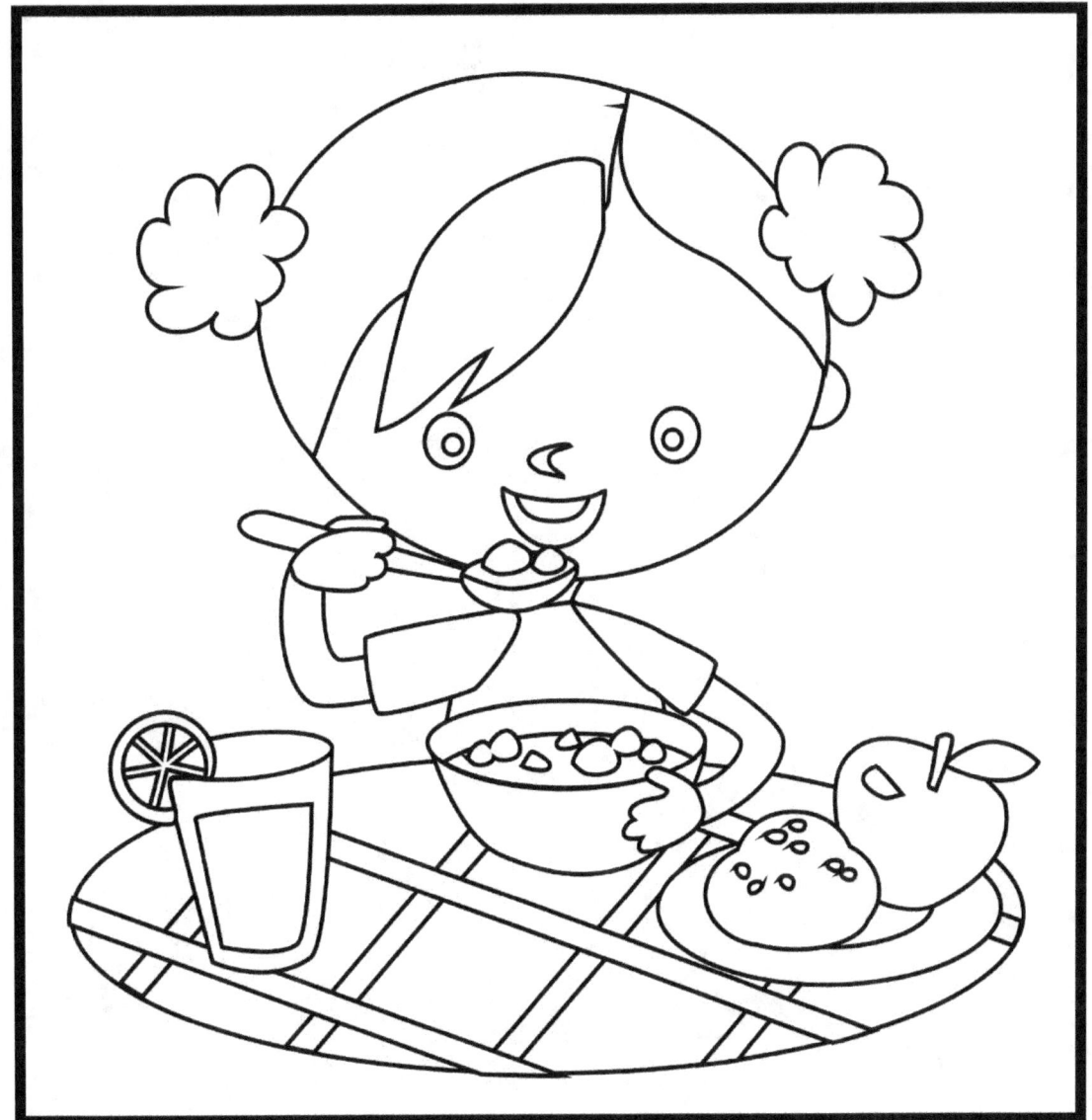

note:

_____

_____

_____

FEBRUARY 43TH

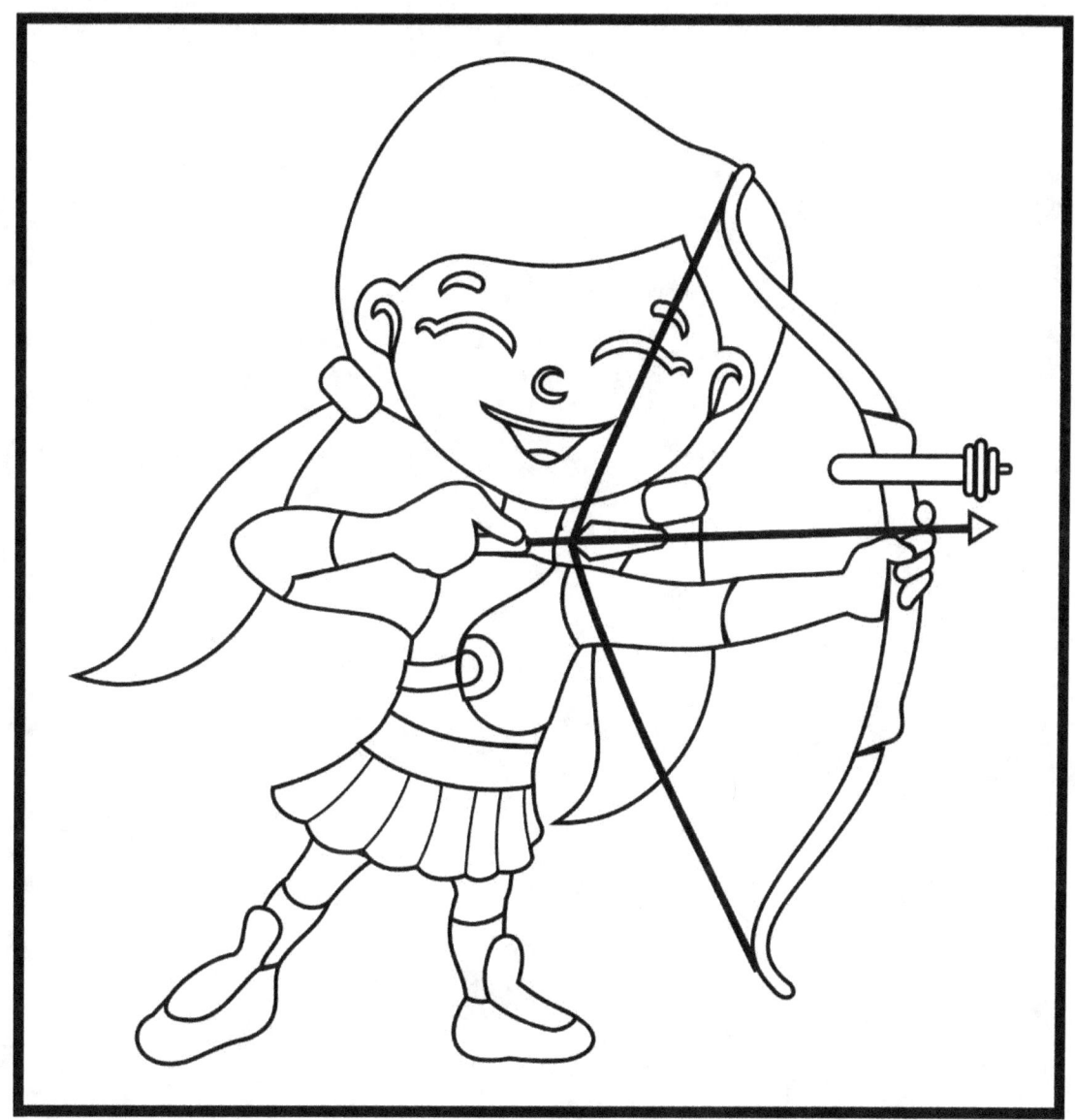

note:

_____

_____

_____

FEBRUARY 44TH

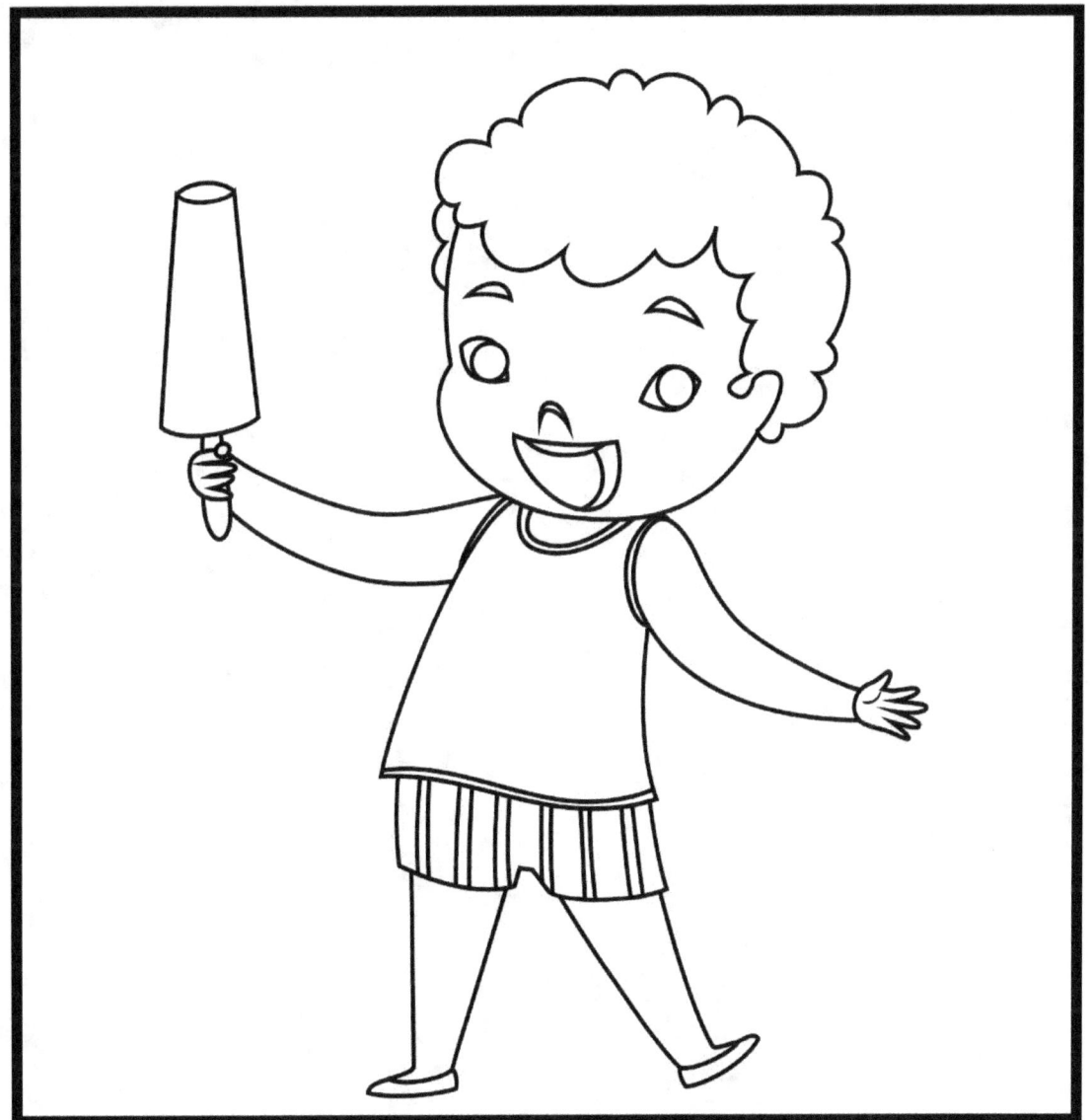

note:

_____

_____

_____

FEBRUARY 45TH

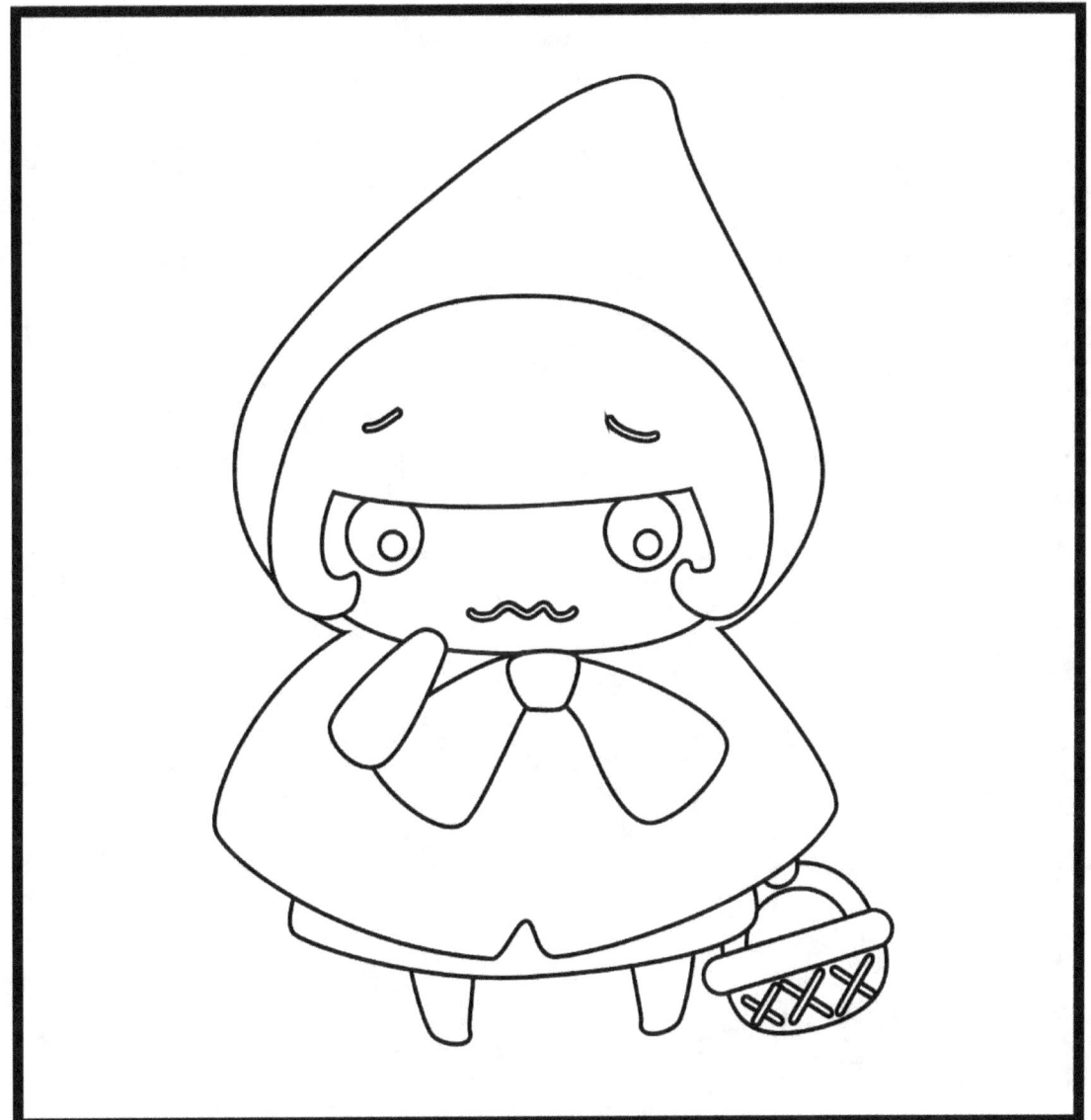

note:

_____

_____

_____

FEBRUARY 46TH

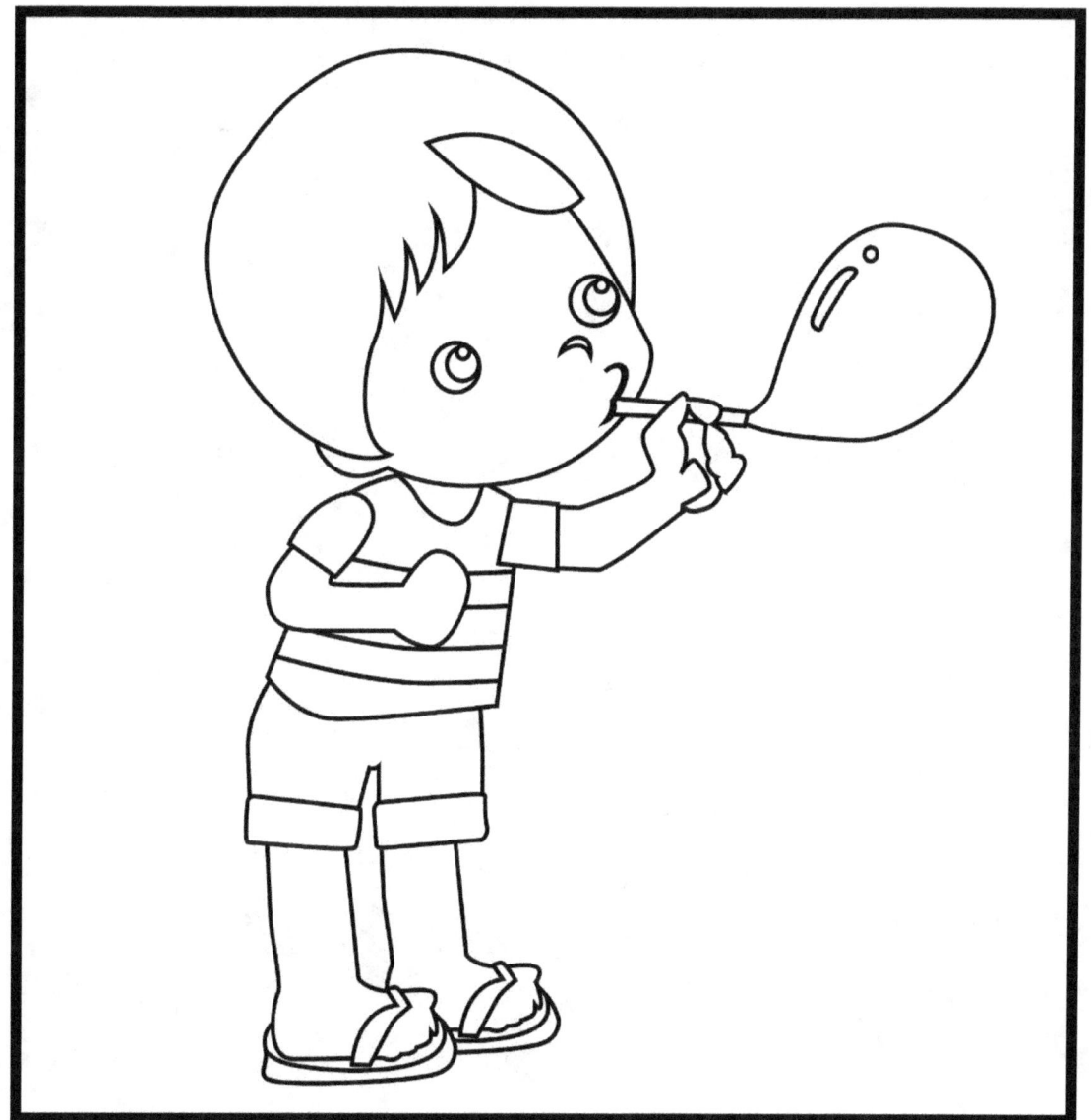

note:

_____

_____

_____

FEBRUARY 47TH

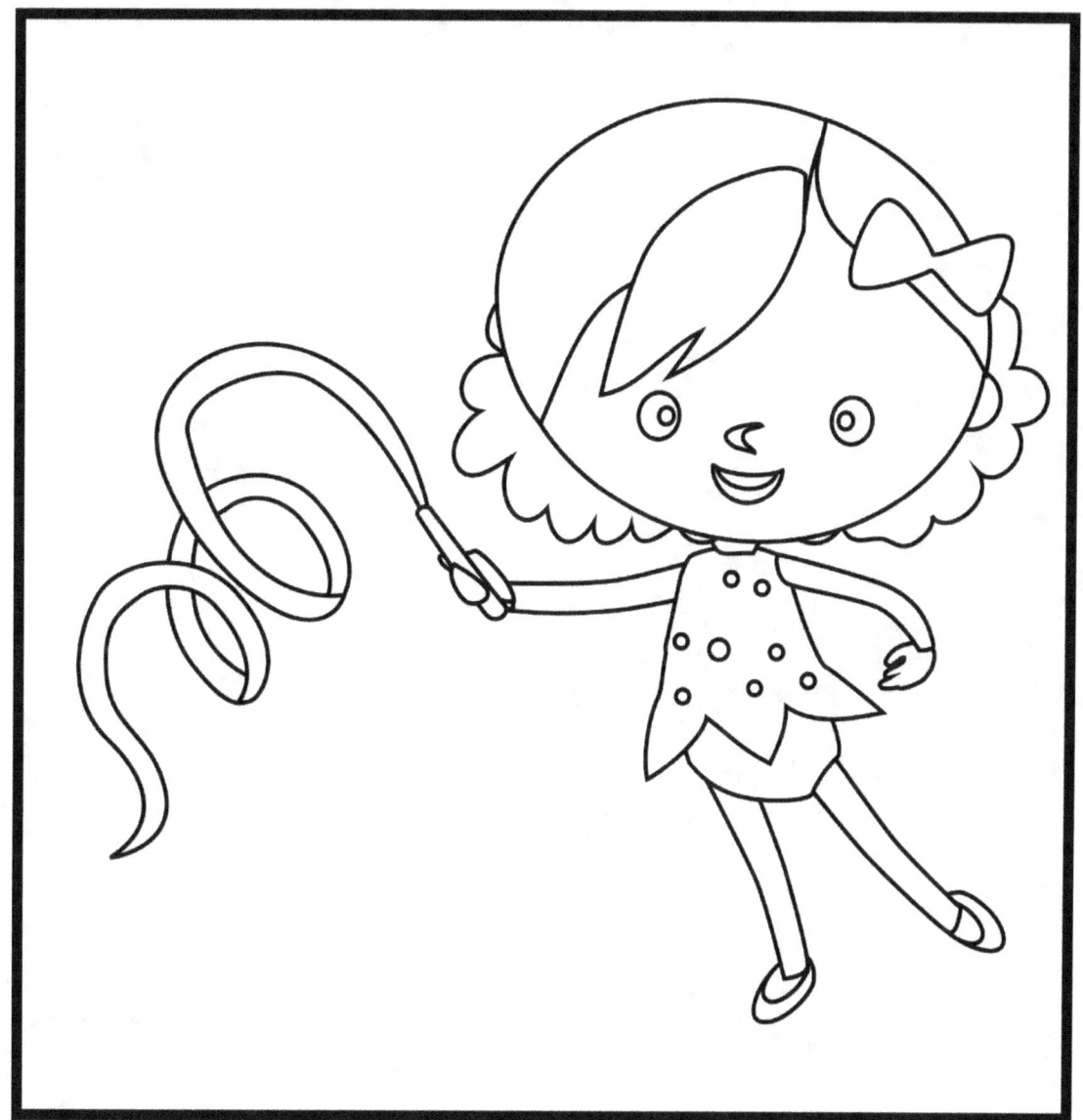

note:

_____

_____

_____

FEBRUARY 48TH

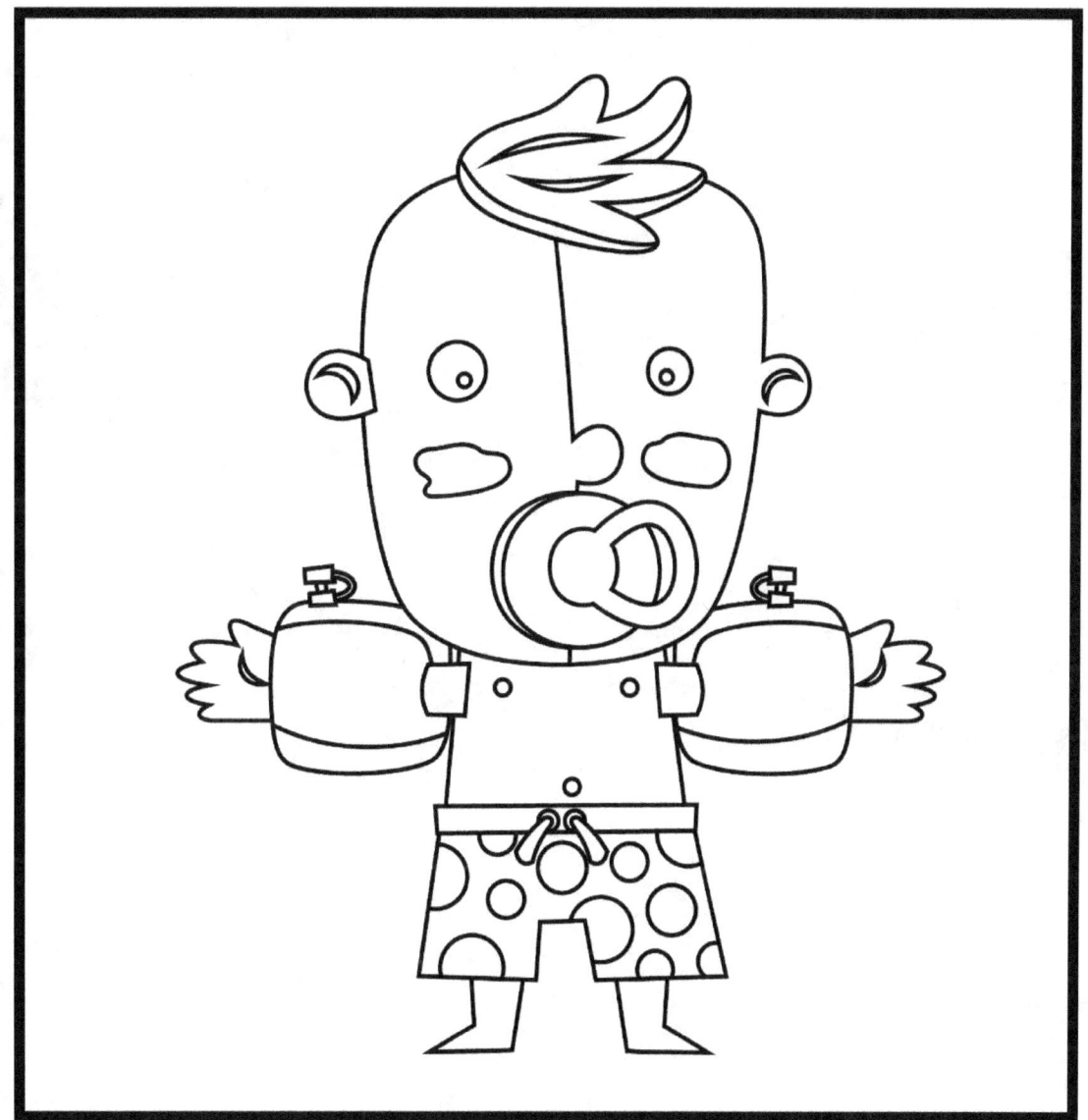

note:

_____

_____

_____

FEBRUARY 49TH

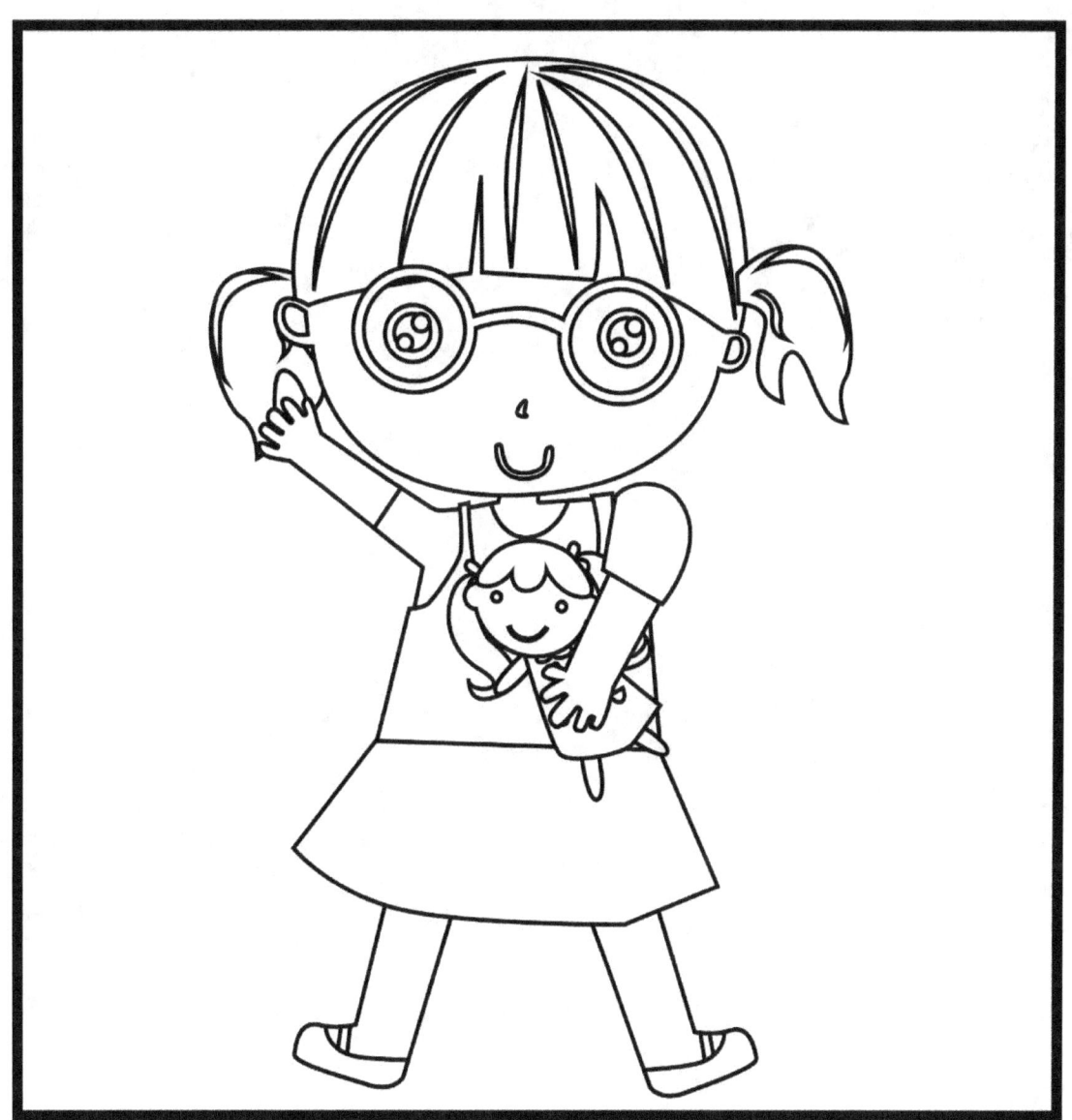

note:

_____

_____

_____

FEBRUARY 50TH

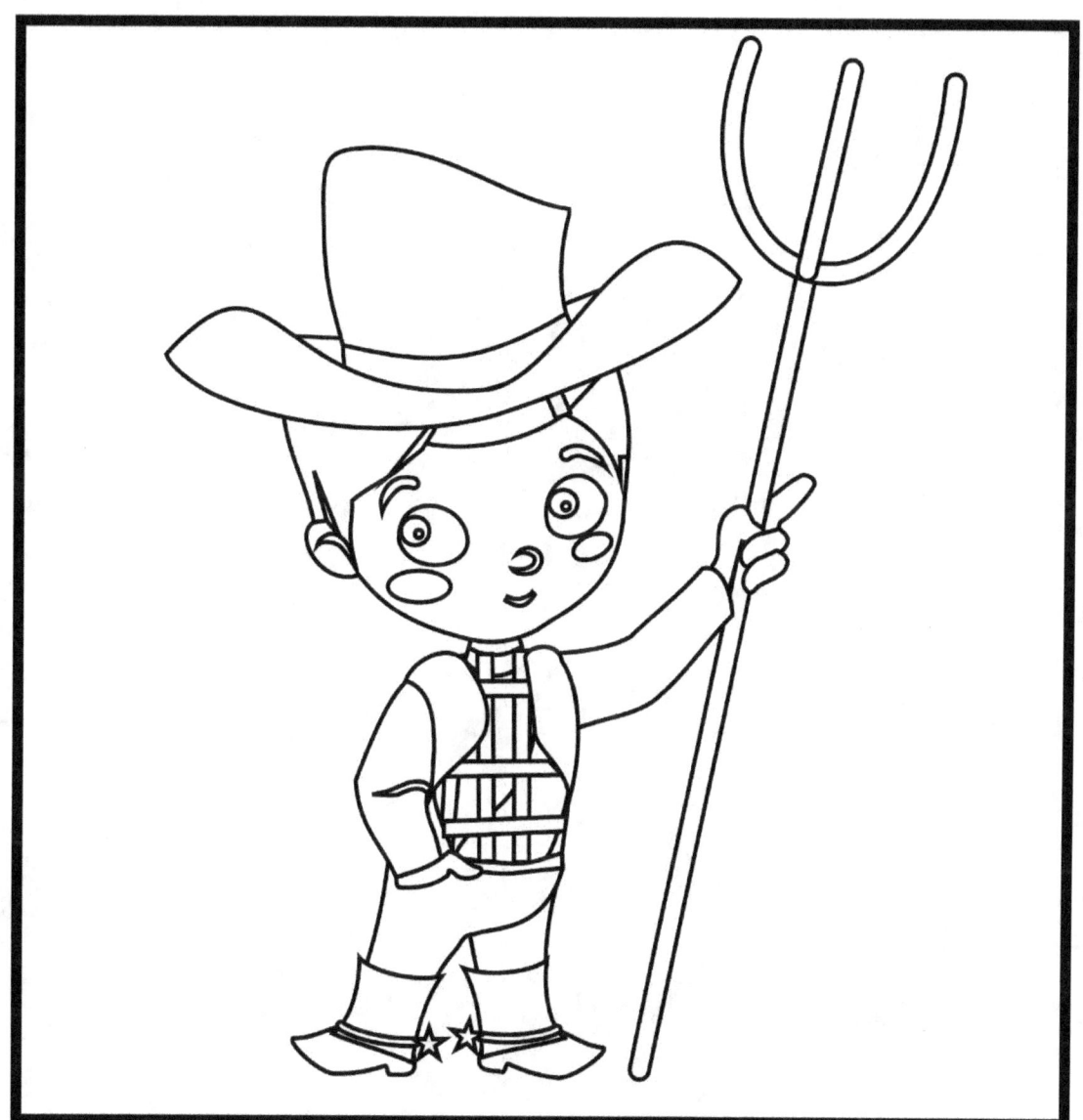

note:

_____

_____

_____

www.ingramcontent.com/pod-product-compliance
Lightning Source LLC
Chambersburg PA
CBHW081605220526
45468CB00010B/2776